The Breaking Point

Copyright © 2023 by Marci Bolden
All rights reserved.

No part of this book may be reproduced in any form or by any electronic or mechanical means, including information storage and retrieval systems, without written permission from the author, except for the use of brief quotations in a book review.

This is a work of fiction. Names, characters, businesses, places, events, locales, and incidents are either the products of the author's imagination or used in a fictitious manner. Any resemblance to actual persons, living or dead, or actual events is purely coincidental.

Cover design by Okay Creations

Print ISBN: 978-1-950348-68-8

The Breaking Point

MARCI BOLDEN

PINK SAND
PRESS

ONE

DESPITE THE WARMTH of the summer afternoon, a chill ran down Taylor O'Shea's spine, and goosebumps rose on her pale skin. Anxiety washed over her the moment she parked her pickup outside the Truman Brothers Funeral Home in the outskirts of Fairfax, Virginia. Taylor didn't do funerals. She didn't do heavy emotions. And she definitely didn't do death.

The urge to drive away grew as she looked at the gray brick building. Inside, one of her best friends was in mourning. Four days prior, Jade Kelly's mother had passed away without warning. Jade had been on an emotional roller coaster since, alternating between calm acceptance and sobbing so hard her entire body shook.

These types of breakdowns were something Taylor was getting slightly better at handling since becoming friends with Jade and Darby Zamora. With that realization, Taylor glanced at her passenger. Darby sat staring at the building too. Though she didn't think Darby had the deep-seated dread Taylor was feeling, her friend looked nearly as uneasy.

Before becoming friends with Jade and Darby, Taylor's circles had mostly consisted of gruff *male* construction workers. She hadn't had much experience with feelings and communication and all the things that, up until the last two years, she'd considered much too touchy-feely for her. Her friendships with Jade and Darby had helped her grow so much as a person, but emotions still made Taylor uneasy.

She was content to stuff them down until they went away. However, this dread wasn't going to go away, and as much as Taylor wanted to run, she would never leave when her friend needed her. She, better than anyone, knew how shitty it felt to get ditched.

"Are you okay?" Darby asked. She had tamed her signature fire-engine-red hair from the usual barrel rolls to a low ponytail, and her heavy makeup was a little more subdued than usual, but the black dress she wore was still the 1950s style she favored.

Though Taylor was more into cargo pants and fitted T-shirts, she'd borrowed clothes from Jade for the funeral. Jade had insisted Taylor not purchase anything for today, but Taylor wished she had. Jade's clothes were a tight fit. Taylor preferred clothes that gave her room to move.

Her straight black hair hung limp over her shoulders and would blend seamlessly into the black blazer she intended to put on once they stepped out of the vehicle.

Darby had insisted Taylor couldn't wear the jacket while driving or it'd be wrinkled. Taylor hadn't argued. The damn thing had felt like a straitjacket when she'd tried it on. The less time she spent wrapped up in it, the better.

Taylor shrugged her shoulders a few times, trying to relax a little. "Is it normal to feel twitchy before these things?"

"For you?" Darby asked. "Probably. For most of us, we just feel sad. Poor Jade. This has been so hard on her."

That was the only reason Taylor had dragged herself to this thing. Before today, the one and only funeral Taylor had ever attended was for her grandfather—the man who had raised her. He probably would have hated having a funeral. He probably would have told her to toss him in a ditch with a six pack and a carton of smokes and let him be. But she'd put her energy into meticulously planning a funeral on the meager budget she'd been able to scrape together.

It hadn't been fancy, but he probably still would have told her it was too much. Too expensive. Too depressing. Just like her, Grandpa had been much more sensible and unemotional than most. He hadn't had much use for sentimentality.

His funeral had been depressing, but the guys from the construction company had told bawdy jokes and drinking stories to lighten the mood. Rather than sitting around crying, they talked about the project they'd been working on when Grandpa had collapsed. The house they had been building was nearly complete when he'd died.

The cancer in his lungs hit him hard and fast. He'd ignored the signs for too long. By the time a doctor diagnosed him, he was close to the end. Taylor suspected he knew he was dying and that was why he never got treatment. He wouldn't have wanted it. They couldn't afford it. And he would have left this world even crankier than he'd been.

Instead of treating the illness, he worked through it until his body gave out. The men at the funeral talked about how that was just like him. And then laughed at how stubborn the man was.

Something told Taylor that wasn't going to happen at this funeral. Jade was super successful and not quite uptight, but she didn't have construction site humor. And she wouldn't be joking about how her mom pushed through because she was too damn hardheaded to do anything else.

This funeral was going to be intense. Serious. Emotional.

"Come on," Darby said, opening the passenger door. The loud creaking raked over Taylor's nerves, mostly because they were already raw but also as a reminder that she needed to fix the damn thing. She'd been so busy with the success of the business she'd started with Jade and Darby almost a year prior that her old truck wasn't getting the attention it needed.

ReDo Realty had come together without much thought or planning. Taylor's construction business was tanking, Jade had recently become a self-employed marketing guru, and Darby had stumbled with one of her businesses and ended up in some hot water. Though her troubles worked out and she closed her business, The UnDo Wedding Boutique, she had laughed at the idea of calling their new business ReDo as an homage to her failure. The name had stuck, and ReDo Realty was born.

They bought their first house, which required a major remodel, and sold it for a huge profit. And so it began. Chammont Point was rapidly growing, and they'd been able to sell their houses almost immediately after updating the rundown properties. Though flipping houses had not been something Taylor had ever considered doing, she'd realized she was good at it. Between her and her friends, they were kicking ass at this business.

ReDo Realty more than made up for Darby's boutique

and Taylor's construction company, and it kept Jade busy with marketing and running the business end of things.

What Taylor wouldn't give to be tearing out cabinets in a rundown house right now. Though she understood this was a thousand times worse for Jade, Taylor's discomfort started bordering on panic. Not just because of the occasion, but it was times like this—when Jade was surrounded by people from her former life—that Taylor realized what an outcast she was compared to her friends.

As Darby walked confidently ahead in her heels and pretty dress, proud to not fit in, Taylor glanced down at her black slacks, gray Vans, and gray blouse. While she'd been able to squeeze into Jade's clothing, Jade's feet were far too narrow. Taylor felt like one of Cinderella's stepsisters trying to squeeze into a pair of Jade's flats.

"Oh," Taylor said. "My blazer." That actually belonged to Jade as well. She trotted back to the truck, pulled the pressed jacket from the backseat, and shrugged into it. When she caught up to Darby, she didn't have to speak.

Darby knew exactly what to do. She stopped walking and skimmed over Taylor before fixing the lapel and smiling sweetly. "You look very nice."

"Thanks," Taylor muttered.

As soon as she and Darby walked inside the funeral home, Taylor felt like the air had changed to something denser. Breathing became much more difficult. Her chest tightened and her stomach knotted.

The air conditioner was blowing, but the atmosphere was stale, and the temperature was almost too cold. Everything about the lobby was staged to be welcoming and comforting, but fresh cut flowers, muted colors, and stiff-looking furniture couldn't take away the overlying feel of the place. Death. This place felt like death. Smelled like death.

Taylor couldn't stand it. She glanced back. On the other side of the glass doors, the sun was shining. The air was thinner. The sky was blue.

"Poor Jade. I remember when my mom died," Darby whispered, drawing Taylor back to the rows of folding chairs. "I was so lost."

"You were eighteen," Taylor managed to say through the tense breath she'd taken. "Jade's an adult. A *strong* adult. And look at all these people here to support her. And she has us. She's better equipped to handle this than you were."

"Still," Darby said and pressed a hand to her heart in the way she did when she was feeling overwhelmed. "She finally found her footing, and now this."

"I know," Taylor said, thinking of Jade's battle with cancer, her divorce, and all the ups and downs when they'd first met. Since then, Jade had started dating a man who seemed to suit her perfectly. She'd been happy over the last year. Really happy.

Now this, as Darby had said.

Taylor glanced around the gathering, looking for Jade's auburn hair in the sea of blondes and brunettes. Her number-one objective in that moment was to let Jade know she was there, once again offer her condolences, and then disappear into a corner where, hopefully, the air was a little easier to inhale.

"Hey," Darby whispered. "Taylor?"

After blinking several times, Taylor focused on bright-red hair and then Darby's concerned dark-brown eyes.

"Whoa," Darby said under her breath. "You're pale. Like...just-saw-a-ghost pale. Let's find you a seat."

The fist clutching Taylor's heart squeezed harder.

She could do this.

She could do this.

She *could* do this.

Shit. She couldn't do this.

Turning, she was about to make a beeline for the door, but then she spotted Jade. She was smiling in that annoyingly understanding and kind way at someone at least twice her age. The woman was crying, and Jade was rubbing her arm, supporting her.

Her mom had just died, but she was supporting someone else. Taylor would be an absolute shit to leave because she was uncomfortable when Jade was trapped there, supporting other people. Taylor and Darby were there to support Jade. That's what she had to do. Her discomfort be damned.

Suck it up, buttercup. That's what her grandpa had always told her when she started to whine about something... anything. *I guarantee someone somewhere has it a hell of a lot worse than you.*

That person, at this particular moment, was Jade. As soon as the elderly woman hugged Jade and moved on, Jade blew out a long breath, and Taylor headed her way.

Despite her insistence that she wasn't a hugger, Taylor wrapped Jade up and squeezed her tight.

Jade smiled when they leaned back to look at each other. "I saw you when you walked in. You looked a bit queasy. How are you doing?"

Taylor swallowed hard and then spoke around the lump resting high in her throat. "I'm supposed to ask you that."

"We can ask each other."

Taylor would have rolled her eyes, but they were frozen wide open. "I'm— I'm okay."

"She's not okay," Darby said softly.

Shooting her a hard glance, Taylor silently warned her to shut up. The last thing Jade needed was to worry about Taylor. She had enough on her shoulders at the moment.

"I can see that."

Taylor dragged a hand over her forehead and realized there was a bit of moisture along her hair line. Cold sweats? Nice. If she took off the blazer she was wearing, she had no doubt there would be dark circles in the armpits. She lamely gestured. "You know…funerals are…tough."

Jade nodded. "Yeah."

Remorse filled Taylor's chest. Why had she said that? Of course Jade knew. She was there because her mother had died. "How are *you*?"

"About the same as you, I guess. I just hide it better."

The guilt in Taylor's gut grew more intense. Jade was putting up such a strong front when she was the one in mourning while Taylor was about to crawl out of her skin. Taylor had no right to feel so intensely out of sorts when Jade was struggling to hold herself together.

Shame tugged at Taylor's heart.

Darby offered Jade a soft coo and took her hand. "We're so sorry for what you're going through."

Jade nodded her head toward the door. "Let's step outside for a few. I could use some fresh air."

Taylor wished she could believe that. Jade was still more concerned with her friend than she was with herself. Jade was like a freaking saint or something—always looking out for other people. Darby was the goofball who came up with off-the-wall antics whenever life got too intense. Taylor was still trying to figure out her role. Darby and Jade would say she was the logical one of the group, the one who kept them grounded. But Taylor felt like a thorn at the moment.

However, as soon as they stepped out into the heat, Taylor was able to take a breath. A *real* breath. She inhaled deeply and huffed the air out as relief found her. Her anxiety eased its hold on her chest, and the feeling that she was about to choke on her own internal organs slipped away.

Jade strolled away from the funeral home, and Taylor and Darby followed her lead. Tall trees shaded the sidewalk and kept the heat at a tolerable level as they walked. "Better?" she asked after several minutes of quiet.

"Yeah," Taylor said, barely loud enough to be heard. "I'm so sorry, Jade. I—"

"Don't apologize," Jade said. "It's hard for me to be in there too."

Taylor looked down and, for some reason, seeing their feet as they walked together felt like a message. Jade and Darby were on either side of Taylor. The black heels that they walked so easily in were classy and…proper for the ceremony. Then there were Taylor's gray canvas slip-ons. The nicest shoes she owned. She should have bought a pair of black flats. Why hadn't she bought new shoes?

Because Jade had told her not to. Jade had told her the gray shoes were fine. Perfect. She said having Taylor and Darby being with her was more important than what they wore.

Taylor frowned as she began to doubt that. She felt out of place and underdressed. She shifted again but did her best to hide her discomfort. Jade shouldn't have to be concerned about Taylor's discomfort. Not right now.

"I don't want you worrying about me right now," Taylor said. "This is your mom's—"

"I know." Jade looked up at the sun and heaved a big breath. "But a funeral is a funeral, and those are always difficult."

"How are you holding up?" Darby asked. "Really?"

Jade nodded slightly. "I'm going to be okay. I really am." She stopped walking and faced Taylor. "I know you came all this way, and I appreciate it so much, but I really do think you should go home."

Jade might as well have punched Taylor in the face. How could she send her away?

"But—"

Putting her hand on Taylor's arm, Jade offered her that irritatingly sympathetic smile again. "I know how hard this is for you. Everything about this is uncomfortable for you."

Taylor scoffed. "It's a funeral, Jade. It's uncomfortable for everyone."

"More so for you. The fact that you tried means *so* much to me, but I don't want you to put yourself through something this upsetting. I have family here to help me."

"I'm not leaving you right now. Are you kidding me? I'm not leaving you right now. *No*," Taylor insisted.

Tears sprang to Jade's eyes, and Taylor shifted on her feet. She might be better at handling emotions and all that, but crying still made her want to turn and run. She looked down and realized that was the point. She wanted to be here for Jade, but the level of discomfort she was feeling wasn't going to make that possible. Supporting her friend was a lot easier when it was relationship issues or business conflicts. Death and all the emotions that went with it made Taylor feel inadequate.

"I have a roomful of people here to help me through today," Jade said. "I have Liam and my boys."

Liam was Jade's boyfriend and definitely would be better at offering Jade comfort and support. But that didn't mean Taylor shouldn't be there. The implication that she wasn't needed sent an unexpected pain through her heart. Her face must have shown it, because Jade quickly spoke up.

"I love that you're here. I love that you came and that you want to be here, but I'm going to be okay. You don't need to put yourself through this for me."

Taylor glanced at Darby, wondering what she would do. Would she leave? Taylor didn't think so, but Taylor didn't always see situations the way others did. She didn't exactly have normal responses. She'd learned young to assess and analyze. Looking for cues and reading body language was second nature to her now. That didn't mean she always knew what to do with what she determined.

Taylor liked to consider herself as rough around the edges, but the reality was she was more than that. She was hard and cold sometimes. But even she knew leaving right now would be selfish. She shook her head. "No," Taylor said, feeling shame creeping up on her. Jade shouldn't be taking care of her. She was supposed to be taking care of Jade. "I'm going to be here, Jade."

"Okay," Jade said softly. "But I want you to know that if you decide to leave, I completely understand, and I promise I won't be upset."

"Thanks," Taylor said. Once again, her guilt swelled in her chest, and she reminded herself this was Jade's grief to work through, not Taylor's. This was Jade's trauma. Not Taylor's. Focus. On. Jade. Reaching out, Taylor took Jade's hand and offered her a soft smile. "I really want you to know that I'm here for you."

"I know you are. I love you for it. We should get back inside, then," Jade said and turned toward the funeral home.

As they walked back toward the doors, Darby started asking Jade what she could do to help, what Jade needed, and all the right things a friend should do in instances like this. Taylor fell a step behind and let Darby do her thing.

Taylor's grandpa had taught her how to build things and take care of vehicles and plumbing, but those things didn't really help much when it came to nurturing people. This was definitely Darby's area, and Taylor was happy to let her have it.

Before long, they were seated in rows of uncomfortable chairs while a preacher spoke about their lost loved one. He told stories that Taylor had never heard, some funny and some sad, but when he started speaking of the love between mother and daughter, Taylor's stomach did a funny flip and acid rose in her throat.

According to the preacher, Jade had been her mother's pride and joy. She never failed to find a way to turn a conversation back to her daughter and grandsons. The mother and daughter had been as close as any pair he'd ever seen, he said.

Taylor glanced toward Jade and watched her wipe her eyes. Taylor couldn't imagine the pain she was feeling. When her grandpa had died, she'd been so messed up that she'd jumped into a horrible relationship with a conman. She'd known he was worthless. She'd known he was a liar. But she'd been on some kind of downward spiral that made her feel like she'd deserved the shit he'd doled out to her.

She hadn't snapped out of the self-destructive phase until it was too late. She'd married the jerk and spent months trying to figure out why. When she'd finally kicked him out, he stole her tools—all that she'd had left of her grandfather, and she'd been devastated. Her grandfather hadn't exactly been an ideal role model, but he'd been the only family Taylor had. Losing his tools was like losing him all over again.

Though Jade was stronger than Taylor and had a much better support system, she did have a history of making bad decisions when life flipped upside down on her. Those decisions weren't as life altering as marrying the wrong man, but even so, Taylor vowed to make sure her friend didn't sink into the same kind of destructive cycle. She'd keep an extra close eye on her.

"The love between a mother and daughter is unbreakable," the preacher said, drawing Taylor's attention back to him, "even in death."

Taylor didn't mean to snort at the statement, but she did and quickly covered it by pretending to wipe her eyes when Darby jerked her face toward her. Certainly, Darby knew Taylor wasn't crying, but others didn't, and Taylor didn't want to be rude.

She hadn't meant to let out a wry laugh at the sentiment

about a mother's love, but she couldn't help herself. Unbreakable maternal love? Maybe Jade had experienced that, but Taylor didn't even know what that meant. Her mother had ditched her when she was six and hadn't been seen since.

Ditched her wasn't exactly accurate.

Susan O'Shea, repeat offender, had been sentenced to four years in prison a few weeks before Taylor's seventh birthday.

Since no one, not even her mom, knew who her dad was, Taylor had been staring down foster care. At the last minute, her mom's father had stepped forward and offered to take her in. Her grandpa had been reluctant to raise a girl alone, but he'd provided Taylor with the most stable home she'd ever known, even if it had been filled with baseball games turned up too loud, too much drinking, and a cussing old man. Which was still a hell of a lot better than her mother had done.

Drugs. Theft. Lies.

Those had been the staples of her early childhood, thanks to her mother. Taylor's first experience shoplifting was when her mother slipped a candy bar into the back of her diaper before carrying her out of a convenience store. Taylor wasn't old enough to remember. She only knew because her mom had told her that story at least once a week until she'd gone away. And she'd laugh every time.

"You were born for five-finger discounts, baby girl," she'd say as if that had been some kind of badge of honor. Taylor supposed it *had* been to her shithead mother.

Though the woman certainly had been released from

prison sometime while Taylor was still a minor, she'd never returned for her daughter. Taylor was better off. She knew that. Even so, she resented the hell out of her mother. Not only for the turbulent years of her young life but for not caring enough to come back.

So no, padre, a mother's love wasn't unbreakable. At least not for all mothers.

Darby elbowed Taylor gently. "Are you okay?"

"Fine. Pay attention," Taylor said, even though she was the one with the wandering mind. Doing her best to force away thoughts of her own mother, she turned her attention on the man beside Jade. Her stepfather slowly stood and made his way toward the podium to give his parting words for his wife.

The knot in Taylor's stomach grew tighter. Man. The emotional shit was about to get real.

Taylor put another log on the fire and watched the sparks scatter. Usually sitting around a fire in the cove made Taylor feel at home, even though she didn't live in the cove with Jade and Darby. The small inlet on Chammont Lake only had room for the two small cabins that they inhabited. If there'd been room for three, Taylor probably would have bought space there by now. Though she loved her privacy, she still felt a twinge of jealousy that her best friends were neighbors.

Even though she didn't live here, she was more at home with Jade and Darby than anyplace else in the world. This night, however, she felt so emotionally drained and on edge. Sitting around the fire with her friends had her wishing she could run to her truck and drive back to the crappy little house she'd been renting for over two years.

Jade and Darby didn't know why she was still renting that borderline shack. They had been telling her it was time to upgrade, but she didn't want to take the time to commit to not only finding a new place but also the hassle of moving.

No. That wasn't exactly true. Every time Taylor looked at a nicer house to rent, part of her started feeling so out of place her skin would start to crawl. From a young age, her mom had told her that one of the most dangerous things a person could do was get too attached to a place. Once someone got attached to a place, leaving was impossible.

Susan O'Shea certainly stood by her word. She was so unattached to everything, she hadn't just abandoned their old home, she'd abandoned her kid.

Though those lessons were far from her mind these days, others weren't so easy to forget. She and her grandfather had shared the same rundown trailer for all the years that she'd lived with him. They hadn't moved around. They hadn't slipped away in the night without paying rent.

But they'd never moved up either. Grandpa had always said they had a roof over their heads. Asking for more was a waste. Needing more was foolhardy. And wanting for more was selfish.

Someone nudged Taylor, causing her to blink several times before turning her eyes to Jade.

"Where'd your mind go?" Jade asked.

"Nowhere. I'm fine. How are you?"

Jade returned her gaze to the fire. "Glad today is over.

Now the real grieving process can begin." She inhaled a deep breath and let it out loudly. "I've been thinking about something."

"What?" Darby pressed when Jade didn't freely give up her thoughts.

"If I get sick again—"

"Don't talk like that," Taylor stated firmly. She hadn't known Jade when her friend had been battling cancer, but she didn't want to even consider that the disease could return.

"I need someone to know what I'm thinking," Jade said. "And it has to be you two. I can't tell my kids these things."

"You can tell us," Darby said softly.

Taylor darted her eyes across the low flames, but Darby didn't make eye contact. Taylor suspected that was intentional. She didn't want to see Taylor's scowl.

"Don't have a funeral for me," Jade said. "Not like the one we had for my mom. It's too depressing. Have a party. Darby, you can cater, and Taylor, you can tell everyone to get their damn drinks off my end tables unless they use a coaster."

Taylor smiled. Jade was constantly snapping at her to use coasters. Taylor tried to remember, but she wasn't used to having furniture worth caring about. Setting her drink down without thinking was a habit she was still working on breaking.

"I want a funeral," Darby said, "but I want everyone to dress in brilliant colors and play nothing but Elvis and Ella and all the greats. But the happy songs. Not the sad songs. I don't want anyone being sad."

Taylor glanced between her friends when they looked at

her as if expecting to hear her desires. "Put me in a canoe and set me on fire. Like a Viking."

Jade chuckled, but Darby rolled her eyes. "We'd all go to jail for destroying your corpse."

"I'll leave cash under my mattress to pay your bail," Taylor said as she lifted her beer to her lips.

"How will we get it?" Darby asked. "We'll be in *jail*."

Taylor swallowed a gulp before grinning. "Guess you'll have to get creative."

"We should have done something different for Mom," Jade said softly. Just like that, the lighter mood around the fire fizzled out, and the gloom returned. "She wouldn't have wanted something so...sad."

"You would have done something else if you'd had more time to plan," Taylor said. "You were caught off guard, Jade. You didn't have time to think outside the box."

"You did right by her, boo," Darby said sweetly. "She would have been happy with the service. It was lovely."

"I know it was, but it wasn't...*her*." Big tears rolled down her cheeks, and Taylor had to turn her focus to her beer. "It wasn't...sunshine and zephyr lilies and coffee on the porch."

"Funerals never are," Darby countered. "When my mom died, I didn't have a clue how to plan a funeral. I just did what the funeral director told me. That was all I could do. Sure, she would have loved if we'd all sat around having a big meal instead of sitting in a cold room crying over her, but that's what we do. Right? That's what we do."

Taylor pressed her lips together and stared into the fire as her mind once again traveled back to her grandfather's funeral. She'd had time to plan her grandfather's funeral, but she still hadn't done anything special. She hadn't even considered it.

She'd never felt guilty about keeping it simple until now, when she was looking back and thinking that she should have put a little more effort into saying goodbye to him. There hadn't been too many people who'd attended the service, and those who did scattered quickly. Stories had been shared during the viewing and then again the day of the funeral; however, as soon as her grandfather's service had ended, the mourners parted ways. Perhaps if she had planned a big lunch, they would have joined her. Maybe, if she'd made a bit more effort, they would have stuck around. Instead, Taylor had gone home to the quiet and mourned in peace. Alone.

She'd always gone through things alone before.

Now, she was learning how to be a friend. Darby and Jade had been good for Taylor. They'd softened the rough edges that Taylor had spent years perfecting as a defense against a world that didn't seem to have a kind moment for her. She'd been born into chaos and uncertainty, and her life never seemed to stabilize for long.

"*Taylor.*"

After blinking several times, Taylor focused on Jade. "Huh?"

"Where do you keep going?" Jade asked. "And don't say nowhere. Your eyes keep glazing over, and you're far too quiet."

A frown tugged at Taylor's lips. "It doesn't matter."

"Obviously it does," Darby commented.

"I should have had a better funeral for my grandpa," she said flatly. "I mean…he was…he wasn't the best grandpa a gal could ask for, but he was the only family I had. I should have done more for him."

"Like what?" Jade asked.

Taylor shrugged. "I don't know. Something. Something more than just put him in the ground and walk away. I didn't know how to..." She looked up at the stars. "He never taught me how to take care of things like that. Yeah, I could change oil by the time I was twelve, and I could hang drywall before I could drive, but he never taught me like...life stuff. Moms are supposed to do that, and...well, you know. My mom was about as useful as a wrecking ball on a submarine."

"She had to have had some good qualities," Darby said.

Taylor looked into the fire and shook her head. "No. None that I can think of."

"I bet she was fun," Jade said softly.

"Fun? I guess if you think being forced to shoplift before you learn to count is fun." As soon as she spat out the words, Taylor clenched her jaw. Regret punched her hard. "Sorry," she muttered. "That just slipped out."

Silence hung over them like a wet woolen sweater, and Taylor's guilt grew.

"Look," she finally said, "I didn't have a mom like you guys. She didn't bake cakes or keep the monsters away at night. She thought running away from her responsibilities was a game. Leaving other people to clean up her messes was her favorite entertainment. I mean...look at what she did to me. She stuck me with some crotchety old man who didn't know the first thing about raising me. If he'd known what to do with kids, Mom wouldn't have ended up the way she did."

She looked at her friends again before shrugging. "I didn't have a family like that, like what you guys had, so no...

Mom wasn't fun. Grandpa wasn't fun. And that explains why *I'm* not fun."

"You're fun," Darby said softly. "In a turd in the punchbowl kind of way."

Taylor gawked at her for a few seconds before a grin twitched at the corners of Darby's lips. "Screw you, Darbs," Taylor muttered.

Darby laughed, and a moment later, Jade joined her. As always, Darby knew exactly when and how to cut the tension in the air. Rather than continue her path of self-deprecation, Taylor sipped her beer and let Darby and Jade do the reminiscing. Their childhood memories were much better than hers anyway.

Though she tried to stay focused, a feeling started nagging at her. She knew this feeling. Every now and then the curiosity grew. The desire for answers tapped her on the shoulder and reminded her that she may never know why her mother had never come back for her. Taylor was pretty good at shooing that need away, but this time the need felt different.

The last two years of hearing the stories of Jade and her mother and listening to Darby reminisce about how her mom seemed to be able to read her thoughts had fed the desire growing in the back of Taylor's mind.

Since coming into Jade's orbit, Taylor had seen how normal functional families worked, and that had started highlighting a void inside her that she'd always been able to ignore. She had a mother out there. Somewhere. A woman who had walked away and never, as far as Taylor knew, looked back.

Normally, Taylor would be able to convince herself that

was all the proof she needed to let that woman go. But lately? Lately the desire to find out why Susan O'Shea had abandoned her daughter was growing. Now that she was supporting Jade through the loss of her mother, that feeling was becoming a need. A need that was starting to feel undeniable.

TWO

TAYLOR HAD DONE what she could to stay focused on Jade the previous afternoon. She'd smiled and nodded and offered words of condolence as Jade reminisced and occasionally wiped away her tears. However, in between reassurances and offering her understanding, Taylor's mind continuously wandered to the raven-haired woman who had taught her how to distract cashiers long enough to nab a few bills from a register.

After leaving the cove, Taylor had gone back to her rundown rental and sat on the couch to watch whatever happened to be on television. However, she hadn't been able to focus on that either.

Memories of her mom kept coming to the surface and dragging Taylor into the past. A past that she had let go of long ago. Or so she'd told herself. She'd spent years telling herself that she was better off. Her grandfather had been far from perfect, but he'd saved her from foster care. He'd saved her from a life of bouncing around until some kind soul took her in.

Unable to sleep, Taylor crawled out of bed before the sun rose and headed to the project she'd been working on. A rundown house two blocks from the beach had been a steal but needed lots of work. She was basically gutting the entire house.

She didn't mind. The sound of a sledgehammer breaking through a rotten two-by-two was like salve for Taylor's nerves. Destruction had always been comforting to her. Probably because she'd been born into turmoil.

Every now and then, usually around holidays and birthdays, Taylor would wonder if that would be the year that she'd get a card or a surprise visit. Even though she knew that would never happen, she always found herself watching the mail a little more closely and peeking out the window a bit more often around those times.

And she always felt a sense of disappointment close in on her when the event passed without word from her mother. She knew better. She'd *always* known better.

Just like she knew better than to let all the talk about the maternal bonds her friends shared get to her. She was happy for them. She was thrilled they had close relationships with their moms.

But, just like she felt a twinge of jealousy at their close living arrangement, she felt an unspeakable twinge when they spoke of their mothers.

Darby's mother loved to cook and clean and provide a nice home. Jade's had been kind and supportive and encouraging whenever Jade tried to overcome something.

Taylor's had been a criminal.

One of her mom's favorite games, as she called them, was for Taylor to stand in an aisle and start screaming hysterically. While everyone in the vicinity was focused on the so-called terrified child, her mom was stuffing her extra big purse full of goods. Then she'd rush to Taylor, swoop her up, and cover her in kisses, pretending to be upset. As she clung to her daughter, she'd rush toward the door, insisting she was far too distressed from nearly losing her child to continue shopping.

Once they were inside her mom's beat-up sedan, Susan would laugh and tell Taylor what a good partner she was. Partner? Taylor had no idea what she was doing. She was a child. Not a partner.

By the time Susan went to prison, Taylor had figured out the so-called games weren't games at all. She felt guilty because she knew stealing was wrong. Not because her mom had taught her that, but deep in her tiny gut she understood right from wrong. Susan had deserved to go to prison. She'd deserved every day she spent locked away from the honest people in society.

So why the hell was that broken and abandoned part of Taylor crying out now? Why the hell was her need to find her mother and demand answers becoming so strong? Her mother had tried to turn her into a criminal. Why would she want to find someone who used a child? Why would she want to find someone who believed it was better to steal from hardworking people than to just get a damn job?

Taylor knew better. Finding Susan would be a mistake, and Taylor knew it. If, by some sick twist of fate, she ever ran into her mother again, it would be a disaster.

Rage built in her chest at the memories, and she slammed the board harder.

She was sweaty and breathless when she finally ran out

of energy and had to stop swinging. Leaning on the sledgehammer for support, she rolled her head back, gasping to fill her lungs.

"That was impressive."

Jolting, Taylor turned around. "Jesus, Darby. Do you want your face bashed in?"

Darby chuckled. "Probably not, but thanks for asking instead of just doing it."

"I told her to wait until you stopped," Jade said, walking in behind her with a box and drink carrier from the local coffee shop they all had agreed was the best in town. Though Jade didn't eat much off the menu, she liked the yogurt and granola they offered.

Taylor always thought she paid way too much for a dish that was mostly fermented dairy products, but that was for Jade to decide.

Thoughts of yogurt went out the window as Taylor let the hammer handle go. "Why aren't you at home resting?"

"Because I was hungry," she said and lifted the box. "Is it safe to eat here?"

Skimming the living room of their latest property, Taylor gestured toward the kitchen. "I haven't started in there."

They followed her into the separate space that always made Taylor cringe. The previous owners liked colors. Bright, bold, not-meant-for-adult-spaces type colors. This room was banana yellow with red cabinets that she couldn't wait to knock down and drag to the dumpster perched in the driveway.

She washed her hands in the sink and then wiped them down the front of her cargo pants. "If you would have called,

I would've met you somewhere for breakfast so you didn't have to come here."

"We did call," Darby pointed out. "Like three times."

"We thought you might be taking your stress out on the reno." Jade cast a sorrowful glance Taylor's way, and her feeling of shame grew. Why was Jade being all concerned about everyone else when she was the one who'd just lost her mom?

Because that was what she did to avoid coping. Jade was hurting, so she was putting that energy into helping someone, and right now, her target was Taylor. Taylor would normally reject the efforts, but she supposed letting Jade work through her grief by focusing on her was the least she could do.

So she accepted the coffee that Jade held out then grinned when she lifted the top off the box. Though she was expecting sugary donuts, the box was lined with blueberry muffins. Taylor's favorite. "Thanks," she said, nabbing one.

"This place is going to be amazing," Darby said after taking a long drink from her iced coffee. "I can't wait to see what you do here."

"It's going to be great," Jade agreed.

Taylor glanced between the two before saying around a mouthful of muffin, "What are you guys doing here?"

Darby held her hands out and looked around them. "Getting a feel for the work you're doing."

Leaning her hip against the cracked linoleum countertop, Taylor swallowed hard. "Bullshit."

"I was worried about you," Jade said. "It's not often that you don't show up at our place first thing in the morning. You got right to work today."

By "our place," Jade meant the cove in general. Taylor usually popped in first thing these days. They'd share coffee and talk about business before they all started their days.

"I thought you'd be taking the day off," Taylor said. That was only part of the truth. The rest was that she hadn't slept well the night before. She'd been moody when she'd finally rolled out of bed and hadn't wanted to share her gloom with anyone else.

"Lies," Darby insisted. "She lies. We should torture her until she speaks the truth."

Taylor frowned at her. "Your outfit is torture enough."

Darby laughed at the poke and twisted side to side, making her neon-yellow poodle skirt dance around her. She wore a black fitted T-shirt and had a matching yellow bandanna wrapped around her hair. "Isn't this amazing?"

"No," Taylor deadpanned.

Jade ignored their banter. They loved to tease each other, but Jade tended to put a lid on it before it could turn too sharp. "You put up a good front yesterday, but I could see you were upset."

"Of course I was," Taylor started.

"More than just because of the funeral," Jade stated, not letting her dance around the real issue. "Your mind was somewhere else, and…"

Darby dropped her silly act and looked equally as concerned. "We think we know why."

Discomfort crawled up Taylor's spine like a spider. Rather than engage, she stuffed her mouth with another bite. "Funerals are upsetting," she said around her mouthful and turned her back on them, pretending to fuss with her coffee cup.

"There was an awful lot of talk about mother-daughter relationships yesterday," Jade said softly.

"Something you didn't really have," Darby added.

Taylor focused much too hard on removing the lid from her cup. "Well, that's nothing new, is it?" she asked.

"Taylor," Jade pressed, joining her at the counter. "Did that upset you?"

Eyeing Jade, Taylor shook her head. "I'm fine."

"Are you?" Jade whispered.

Damn it. That was the stupidest question, the easiest to blow off, but it landed like a punch to Taylor's gut. Her throat tightened as she tried to swallow her breakfast down. She nearly choked on the muffin. "Yeah," she breathed when she finally could.

"I don't think you are," Jade pressed.

Taylor looked to Darby with a silent plea to do something ridiculous and distract them all.

Instead, Darby offered her a sweet smile. "The mom thing got to you, huh?"

Scoffing as if that were the most ridiculous thing she'd ever heard, Taylor stepped around Darby to open the box Jade had set aside. She eyed the three remaining muffins, trying to determine which one had the most blueberries. "How many of these are mine?"

"All of them," Darby commented. "But only if you tell us what's bothering you."

"I told you—"

Darby grabbed Taylor's wrist before she could snatch another pastry. "Tell us the truth. Why were you here knocking out walls so early? Why didn't you come by for coffee this morning? And why the hell did you decide gray cargo pants are a real thing?"

Taylor frowned at her friend. "Nobody wearing a poodle skirt in this century gets to talk to me about my fashion choices."

Jade joined them. "Taylor? Tell us what's going on."

She frowned and crossed her arms, her second helping forgotten. "Sometimes, more since you lost your mom..." She rolled her eyes to the ceiling. "Like, you two just keep talking about how great your moms were, and..." An unexpected surge of something she couldn't identify rolled through her chest and left her feeling empty inside. "I'm glad you guys had awesome moms and all that, but..."

"But you didn't," Jade said.

Taylor shrugged dismissively and grabbed another muffin. "It's not a big deal."

"It is," Darby said. "We didn't mean to make you feel bad."

"You didn't," Taylor insisted as she stared at the chunks of granulated sugar on top of the muffin she'd selected. "I mean..." After blowing out her breath, she looked at Jade. "You just lost your mom. You need to talk about her. You need to talk about how much she meant to you, and Darby's a great person for that. I just...I don't have stories like that, you know? Like, I can't...I don't relate, and I don't know what to say when you guys start talking like that, but that's not your fault," she was quick to add. "You can't avoid talking about having a great mom just because I didn't. I get that."

Jade rested a hand on Taylor's arm, and Taylor realized she was rambling. Of course she was rambling. She felt like an ass. Who tells her friends they shouldn't talk about having great parents?

"Thank you for listening to me talk about my mom," Jade said. "I'm sorry that we didn't think about how that would impact you."

Rolling her eyes, Taylor sighed. "Don't be sorry, Jade. I don't want you to be sorry. That's why I didn't say anything. Besides, it's not..." She let her words trail again. Damn it. Why was it so hard to speak like a normal person?

Taylor took a drink of too-hot coffee and concentrated on the way it burned down to her stomach so she could try to get her head on straight. "All this talk about moms and relationships and all that. It's set me on edge." Setting her cup aside, she held her breath and debated if she should tell them what she'd been thinking. "I want..."

"What?" Darby pressed.

"I think..." Taylor's words once again trailed. She stood quietly for several seconds before trying again. "I think I need to find her."

Darby gasped and pressed her hand to her chest as she widened her eyes. "Taylor?"

"I need to find out why she did what she did. I need to know why she never came back for me. Like, was it her or was it me?"

"It wasn't you," Darby was quick to say. "I don't need to know her to know it wasn't you, Tay. Your mom was...not good."

Taylor frowned. "Even *not good* moms don't just leave their kids and never go back."

"Are you sure?" Jade asked. "I mean...you already know

she's not the kind of mom you wanted. Maybe it's best to let it go."

Taylor considered the idea for one more moment before frowning. "No. I need to find her. It's time."

Stupid.

That was the word that continually rolled through Taylor's mind from the moment she uttered the dumbest words to have ever left her mouth. Taylor hadn't stopped kicking herself in the ass since breakfast when she'd confessed that she wanted to find her mom earlier in the day.

Despite their reservations, Darby and Jade had offered to help. They insisted on it, actually. They didn't want her to go through this alone. That's what they'd said. If Taylor were more emotional, she probably would have cried with relief and out of fear.

What if they found out something really terrible? What if they learned things that made them start to wonder if Taylor was like her mom? Maybe they'd start doubting her as much as she doubted herself.

She didn't think she could stand that.

She'd beaten the hell out of the walls at the remodel, but she still hadn't stopped replaying that moment and all her fears over and over in her head.

Now, hours later, sitting at Jade's dinner table, Taylor couldn't focus on anything else. As Jade pulled a casserole out of the oven and Darby fussed about setting the table, a rock sat firmly in the pit of Taylor's stomach because she'd set something in motion that she couldn't decide if she should stop or not.

If she told her friends she'd changed her mind, she knew they wouldn't bother looking for Susan O'Shea. They'd respect Taylor's wishes. The laptops sitting on Jade's coffee table were like flashing neon lights. Darby had brought hers over and set it next to Jade's so they could both dig into research.

As much as Taylor didn't want to constantly look at the computers, her attention kept turning toward them while dinner was served. Jade had insisted that only *after* eating a meal could they sit on the couch and get to work. Which was more like cyber stalking.

Jade had a way of finding people online that she attributed to her former job. Taylor liked to remind her that she had been a marketing executive, not a private investigator. But nobody could deny Jade had scary good search skills. And she had insisted that if Taylor were going to go online snooping around her mom's life, she and Darby would be allowed to do the heavy lifting.

What that had meant, in Jade lingo, was that she wanted to dig up the dirt so she could be the one to break whatever bad news she found to Taylor. That way she could find all the skeletons and dust them off before presenting them to Taylor in a nice little package to soften any impending blows.

While Taylor appreciated Jade's tact, she wasn't burying her head in the sand. There was no use sugarcoating things. The last time she'd seen her mother, the woman was headed to prison. Sure, some people were reformed by facing those consequences, but something told Taylor her mother had just added a few new tricks to her trade. She'd probably made friends with every crook she could find to get pointers.

Darby drummed her fake nails on the table. "Taylor. Pay attention."

"What?" Taylor asked.

"We're going to eat first," Jade said, as if she knew what was going through Taylor's mind. "Then we'll start looking around online."

Sitting back as Jade put a plate in front of her, Taylor stared at the casserole. "What's in this?"

"Mom's neighbor made it," Jade said, sinking into the chair next to Taylor.

Taylor poked at the food on her plate and watched cheese stretch several inches before breaking with a snap. "That doesn't answer my question."

"Chicken and spinach," Jade said.

Darby poked at her dinner as well before taking a forkful and sniffing it. "And...cream of mushroom soup? I'm pretty sure that's cream of mushroom."

Taylor watched as Darby shrugged and then ate the first bite. When she didn't spit it out or offer up any other dramatic show, Taylor took a bite too. The casserole wasn't the best thing she'd ever eaten, a little lumpy and slightly bitter from the overabundance of an unknown spice, but she'd definitely eaten worse. She'd spent the better part of her elementary years eating bologna and mustard on white bread that stuck to the roof of her mouth with every bite. She had no idea what was wrong with that bread, but it had always tasted like glue. Mustard had done little to change that.

Mustard had been a bad attempt at making the

sandwiches easier to tolerate. Kind of like how Jade was going to try to make whatever she found about Susan O'Shea easier for Taylor to swallow. No matter how much mustard Jade squirted on it, the reality of what her mother had been up to all this time was still a gross piece of lunch meat slapped between two gummy slices of bread.

That thought was about as unappealing as the casserole.

"Jade?" Liam called from the back of the small house. "What's that smell?"

Taylor snickered as she poked at her food, however a few moments later, footsteps trudged into the open area. She glanced over her shoulder as Liam walked in, surprised to see someone right behind him.

"Hey," the stranger said. "We haven't met yet. I'm Finn. A friend of Liam's."

Taylor looked from his unkempt hair and five o'clock shadow to the rough hand he was holding out. She wasn't sure if those callouses were from hard work, but if he was a friend of Liam's, the likelihood was that they were from holding a paddle of some kind. "I didn't know Liam had friends," Taylor said, shaking the man's head.

He threw his head back and laughed, causing Taylor to grimace at the loud noise before pulling her hand away.

"What kind of name is *Finn*?" she asked.

"Liam and I were born to fine, strong Irish parents. Not the same parents, mind you. We grew up in the same neighborhood, though. Got in a lot of trouble back in the day." He said in a way that implied he missed the good ol' days. He offered her a smooth smile that made her want to punch him.

"It's some kind of...something," Jade said, distracting

Taylor from the weirdo standing a few feet away. "Take it. I don't think we'll be having seconds."

"Nope," Darby said looking at her plate.

"Doubtful," Taylor added.

The men took the casserole and two forks, not bothering with plates, as they headed back to wherever they'd come from.

"Who is that?" Taylor asked.

"Finn," Darby said, "Liam's friend. He introduced himself."

Taylor resisted the urge to toss her napkin at Darby. "Why is *Finn* here?"

"He had planned some time here on the lake before... everything happened," Jade said uneasily. "He offered to cancel, but there was no point in that. Liam needed help at the shop."

"What about Parker?" Taylor asked. Parker had been helping Liam out at his water equipment rental store for years.

"She's still there, but things are picking up all over Chammont Point," Jade said. "Not just real estate. Everything is getting busier here."

Taylor looked at her food. That was great news for all the local businesses, including theirs, but the idea of the quiet town rapidly growing into something else unsettled her. She liked the quiet, but she couldn't do a damn thing to change what was coming.

"What are you going to do if we find her?" Darby asked.

Taylor's stomach twisted when the subject turned back to her mother. "I don't know," she admitted. "I haven't decided."

"I guess a lot of that depends on where she is," Jade said. "And what she's doing."

Taylor stabbed a chunk of meat. "I know." The food on her plate hadn't exactly been appetizing before, but it suddenly lost what little appeal it'd had. She put her fork down and sat back. "I don't have some stupid, childish fantasy that she's somehow turned into some wonderful person. The reality is, if she'd turned her life around, she would have come for me. She was sentenced to four years in prison. Which means she got out when I was ten. Or she should have. Yet, she never came for me. So don't worry, Jade. I don't have some misguided expectation that she's turned into more than a woman who abandoned her kid."

"Okay," Jade said with a soft voice. "I just want to protect you. You know that, right?"

Taylor smiled and nodded. "I appreciate it."

"You still have us," Darby said, and then she looked at Jade as if to confirm what she was saying. "No matter what happens. You'll always have us."

Taylor smiled. "Thanks. You guys are the best." She pushed her plate away, no longer able to pretend she wanted to eat the weird combination. When she looked up again, Darby was subtly nodding her head at Jade, who in turn, subtly shook her head.

The unspoken but obvious gesture implied that Jade needed to say something and Darby was tired of waiting for it. At first, Taylor thought Darby was encouraging Jade to pull Taylor from her daze, but then Jade shook her head slightly, as if to silently communicate that now wasn't the time.

An entire conversation passed between them via widened eyes and frowns. The bottom of Taylor's stomach dropped out. She immediately assumed something had happened. Something bad. Probably with their business. Things had been going so well, it was only natural that something—likely something huge—was to go wrong now. Things never went smoothly for Taylor. She was used to tripping up. She anticipated tripping up. That was why she was so careful in the decisions she'd made and why she was so frustrated with herself for the random request she'd made earlier in the day.

The fear in her chest grew. She hated when self-doubt got hold of her. Shaking those feelings off had never been easy for her. The feeling of not belonging ran so deep that it tended to be her go-to response. Even now, after years of friendship and Jade and Darby standing by her time and again, Taylor's fear that they would somehow decide she wasn't worthy started to swell.

She was Susan O'Shea's daughter, after all. Daughter of an ex-con. Granddaughter of a cranky old man. Failed business owner.

She was nothing like her friends, and part of her always worried that someday they would decide they didn't like that about her.

Darby liked to say Taylor was made of doom and gloom, but the reality was, Taylor simply liked to be prepared for the inevitable. And right now, that inevitable seemed like the downfall of her, thus far, incredibly successful partnership with her best friends. The only way to go was down, and she'd been dreading the day their company crashed and burned.

She'd already rolled about a hundred worst-case scenarios through her mind in preparation before muttering, "Oh, no. What?"

"What?" Jade asked and cocked a brow at Darby.

Darby batted her doe eyes. "What?"

Taylor sat back. The dread grew with every passing second. It was bad. So bad neither of them wanted to say it. "Guys, what's going on?"

"Jade has something to tell you," Darby said.

Gawking at her, jaw slack, Jade scoffed. "Why do *I* have something to tell her?"

Darby let out a disgruntled sound of her own. "Because *you* did it."

"We," Jade countered. "*We* did it."

"*Guys*," Taylor nearly yelled. "What did you do?"

Letting her shoulders sag, Darby batted her eyes in a show of innocence that Taylor didn't buy. "We kind of... I mean, we..."

"We spent some time this afternoon doing a little research—"

Taylor widened her eyes. "You were supposed to wait for me."

"I know," Darby said with her signature whiny tone. While that usually won points with Jade, it irritated Taylor. "But...we wanted to make sure..."

"We didn't want you to get blindsided by something," Jade stated in her perfectly logical tone.

Even that irritated Taylor at the moment. They had a plan. One that they'd agreed upon. She was going to sit with them and sort through whatever they found to determine what was and wasn't relevant. She'd spent all afternoon bracing herself for that, and they just...jumped in without her.

"Well," she finally said, "what did you find?"

"Your mom. We found your mom," Jade said.

The room suddenly felt like a vacuum. There was no air left to breathe, and everything was pressing down on Taylor. She couldn't even swallow. She tried to ask for clarification, because she'd most certainly misunderstood, but she couldn't speak.

"And?" Taylor hesitantly asked. "What has she been up to?"

"Nothing too bad," Darby quickly insisted. "She's not in prison or anything."

Jade offered her a weak smile. "I did a search and found out there are a lot of Susan O'Shea's out there. But ours...*yours*...is in Arizona. Tempe, to be exact. She's a bartender at this little *slightly* rundown bar and grill."

"We found her address," Darby said.

Taylor creased her brow but didn't ask. Even if Jade explained the ins and outs of how she found all this information, Taylor probably wouldn't understand. She avoided computers and the internet as much as she could.

"She lives in an apartment complex that looks like it was built in the 1960s," Darby said. "Usually, that would be a compliment coming from me, but this time...not so much. We did an online tour through the property management page. They tried to make it look nice, but it's...old and...dirty."

Jade widened her eyes as if to warn Darby to shut up. Darby hadn't meant harm. Taylor knew that her friend had simply been stating a fact.

"She's still a loser," Taylor said. "Is that what you mean?"

"Well..." Darby stated and blew out a long breath.

"Well," Jade offered, "maybe...a little down on her luck at

the moment. The bar where she works seems to be pretty small, and the apartment complex looks like it could use some work. But we don't know for certain. I mean, we haven't been there, and you know how things can look completely different in person than online."

Taylor appreciated the pep talk but didn't believe it any more than either of her friends seemed to. Darby's forced smile sat frozen on her lips, and Jade's maternal tone was encouraging as if to convince a preteen to try out for the cheerleading team just one more time.

Finding her mother had been a mistake. She'd known that from the moment she'd uttered the words. But it was done now. The proverbial genie was out of the bottle.

Taylor looked between the two. "How did you find her so fast?"

"Social media makes finding people easy." Standing, Jade grabbed a folder off her kitchen counter. "I printed off some photos and the information for the bar where she says she works." Sitting at the table, she held her research close. "Do you want to see what I found?"

Taylor stared at the folder like it was a rattlesnake waiting to strike. Her heart started to pound, and a chill ran down her spine. The hair on the back of her neck and along her arms stood on end as if her instincts were screaming for her to run away. Fast and far. But she was stuck to her chair. She had a distinct feeling that if she even attempted to stand, her knees would fail her and she'd fall back, so she didn't even try.

The thin manila folder tucked against Jade's chest seemed benign in and of itself, but the contents had the potential to be explosive. The research Jade had been doing on Taylor's mother was inside. For some reason, Taylor thought the folder should be thicker. There should have been more information, more details, more...something.

The folder didn't seem to be holding much considering her mother would be in her mid-fifties by now.

"Do you want to see this now or after dinner?"

"You can wait," Darby said. "You don't have to open it now. We can finish dinner, maybe have a drink or ten, and then you can open it. If you're ready."

Taylor considered the incredibly appealing option before holding her hand out. When Jade hesitated, she wriggled her fingers to indicate she wanted the file. Jade hesitantly handed it over, and Taylor took a deep breath before flipping the top open.

Her heart did a weird nosedive thing in her chest. There, on the very first page, she found a photo of her mom. The woman's long black hair was streaked with gray at her right temple, and her eyes had lines around them. Creases between her arched eyebrows were deep like the parentheses lines around her mouth. A memory flashed through Taylor's mind—long black hair blowing in the wind, a gravelly voice saying her name, and the smell of baby-powder-scented perfume mixed with cigarette smoke as she sat in the back of a beat-up car with the windows down.

Taylor only had a handful of memories like that, but they were clear in her mind. Seeing a photo of Susan O'Shea brought them all back. Taylor suddenly felt sad. Now that she was older, she was able to fully understand what her life had been. The innocence of childhood had prevented her from understanding that her mom shouldn't have been drinking from that bottle while driving her kid around. She hadn't understood she was too young to be taking cigarettes from her mom's hand and snubbing them out because the woman fell asleep—or passed out drunk—yet again while smoking. And she had only begun to understand that throwing fits in the aisles of stores so her mom could stuff her purse full of items off the racks had been wrong.

Sinking back in her chair as all that came rushing back made her want to cry for the child she'd been. She wasn't a crier. She never had been, but at this moment, tears stung the backs of her eyes, and she had to blink rapidly to ease the sensation.

"She's pretty," Darby offered lightly. "You look like her."

"I'm not like her," Taylor barked. Almost immediately she shook her head sharply. "Sorry. That...that wasn't... I didn't mean to snap."

"It's okay."

"No, it's not." Taylor offered her friend a weak smile. "This is a lot for me to process but that doesn't mean I can be short with you." After looking at the photo again, Taylor took a breath. "I do look like her. You're right. And she looks like my grandma. I remember thinking that when I saw pictures after I went to live with Grandpa. Mom and Grandma looked so much alike. And I look just like them now."

"No," Jade said with a gentle firmness, "you look like *you*. You look like someone who has overcome a lot to get to where she is today."

Taylor ignored the attempt at boosting her morale as she brushed her fingers over the image. "She didn't have to live like she did. She didn't have to end up in prison. She made choices. Bad choices. All the time. I think she liked that," she added thoughtfully as she tried to understand her memories of the woman in the photo. "I think she liked the excitement of doing bad things to see if she would get caught. I never understood why."

"Some people are like that," Jade said. "You can't understand it, Taylor. All you can do is accept that's how she was. That doesn't mean she still is like that."

Usually, Taylor hated when her friend tried to pacify her with her sunshiny outlook, but in this instance, she'd let it pass. She appreciated Jade trying to make this situation easier for her.

"I read that being a thief is like drugs," Darby explained. "You get a high from the chemicals your brain releases at the risk. There's like science behind it and stuff."

If prison had the ability to reform, Taylor hoped it had worked that magic on her mom.

Though she resented that her mom never came back for her, she did hope she had her head on straight by now. Sure, Darby was right. Just because Susan was a bartender didn't mean she was still wild and irresponsible. If she was holding a job, no matter what it was, that was a huge step up from where she'd been the last time Taylor had seen her—being shipped off to prison.

But what if she hadn't changed? What if she was the same lying, cheating, thieving mess she'd been thirty years ago?

Taylor wasn't sure she was prepared to face that. Closing the file, she looked at Jade. "Anything else?"

"Not yet, but we wanted to make sure you really wanted to do this."

Taylor stared aimlessly for several seconds. "I need to know. But I don't know what I want to do with what we find out."

"Okay," Jade said. "We can keep digging, then. I saved links to her social media. We can find out more."

Taylor nodded.

"Do you, um..." Darby started. "Do you care if we order pizza while we look? Because this casserole is the grossest thing I can ever recall eating?"

Jade laughed. "It's horrible."

"Terrible," Taylor agreed. She smiled when Jade gathered the plates and Darby picked up her phone without a second thought. Though she was terrified about what they might find, she was so thankful that they were there with her.

THREE

TAYLOR YANKED with all her might, once, twice, a third time, but the last bit of red cabinetry wouldn't give. She'd managed to knock the majority of the atrocity down, but there was one section left, and no matter how hard she hit or yanked, the damn thing didn't budge. Sweat ran down her spine, tickling her skin until it soaked into the waistband of her pants. That should have been a sign for her to rest, but she was running strong on caffeine and a piss-poor mood.

She hadn't slept well the night before. Her dreams turned to nightmares, which she always woke to realize were just bad memories. As Jade and Darby had found more and more information on Taylor's mom, Jade had made notes that she ultimately printed off and handed to Taylor with a soft smile.

By three a.m., Taylor had the bullet points memorized.

Name: Susan O'Shea
Age: 56
Address: 8328 Eblen Street, Number 25, Tempe, Arizona
Place of Work: Sunkissed Bar and Grill

Jade had also listed three other addresses where Susan

had resided. Three that she could find. Darby had scoured the social media pages of some of the friends tagged on Susan's pages. None of them seemed to be concerned about living by social norms. On one hand, Taylor understood and respected that. On the other, it seemed to be a giant red flag warning her to stay away.

Her mom couldn't have changed that much if she was still running with the same type of people Taylor vaguely recalled from her childhood. She remembered spending way too much time with people who were too busy having a good time to care about the consequences of their actions.

She might have only been six, but even Taylor understood there should have been rules, and the adults around her shouldn't have been breaking them.

At six, she'd had a stronger sense of right and wrong than her mother. She'd had a conscience that had made her feel sick to her stomach every time her mom took her to a store and whispered, "Do your thing, baby girl."

Taylor had only refused the request once. Thirty years later, she could still recall the heaviness of the guilt her mother had put onto her shoulders. How would they eat? What would they wear? How would they get by if Taylor didn't take part in the scheme? Of course, her mother hadn't called it a scheme. She'd said it was a game, but Taylor had known better.

As a child, she'd had more goddamn common sense and decency than her mother.

She had no doubt that she still did. She had no doubt that her mom was still the same piece of shit she'd been back then. So why in the ever-loving hell was she putting herself through this? Why had she sat next to Darby and Jade for two hours the night before looking over every bit of information they could find on Susan O'Shea, trying to determine if it was *their* Susan O'Shea and what that meant for Taylor?

If it would mean anything for Taylor.

Which it shouldn't. She shouldn't allow it to mean anything.

In fact, she should have just burned the folder without looking at it. She should have burned the photos inside before they had a chance to burn into her mind. But the memories had seared into her brain like a branding iron. She'd let them. It was too late.

She'd given into the nagging that used to come and go, and now her mom had a hold of her again. She was real now. Not just some memory that Taylor could brush off. She was no longer a shadow. She was there, front and center, and in the wee hours of the night, Taylor had memorized the lines that had aged her face.

That had been foolish.

That had been stupid.

But she'd done it, and it couldn't be undone. After that, every time she closed her eyes, she saw the woman's face.

Grabbing her sledgehammer, Taylor ground her teeth and eyed the last bit of resistance on the wall. After testing her grip on the handle, she let out a scream and swung. The sledgehammer made contact, and the remaining red woodwork flew across the room, landing with a thud.

"That's what you get, you fucker," she spat at the broken boards and dropped the sledgehammer carelessly.

"You tell 'em, boss," came a casual comment from the kitchen door.

She turned in time to see the man she'd hired to help her with demo three days ago. He'd worked with her on a project previously, and she'd vowed to never hire him again. But she'd needed help and refused to contract a permanent crew until ReDo was at least in its second year of business. She'd learned from her own construction company how quickly the tides could turn. She didn't want people relying on ReDo for full-time employment until the business was at least a year old and steadily making income. Instead, she hired as-needed workers. The list of hard workers was short, and Brad wasn't on it.

But now she needed someone to help with some heavy lifting. The kitchen appliances needed to go, and she had some supplies to move. She needed an able body, and Brad had answered.

"You're late," she told him.

"There was a line at the coffee shop."

She frowned at him. "You either show up on time or you don't show up. I won't be paying you for hours you weren't working."

He gave her a weak salute. "What do you need me to do?"

She gave him a list, and then left the room with another sledgehammer. His arrogant attitude was adding to the rage boiling in Taylor's chest. But as much as he pissed her off, she needed his muscle. She wasn't going to run him off until she'd gotten what she needed.

The dining room of the remodel was bare down to the studs, so she headed down the hall to the bedrooms. The smallest of the three rooms was pink. A little girl's room.

Though the carpet was stained and the walls dinged, she

imagined the kid who had slept there had felt safe. Protected. Wanted.

That kid had probably never lived out of a backpack because her mom was always ready to run. She'd probably never been too scared to play with the few toys she'd had out of fear they'd somehow get left behind. Taylor had a teddy bear that she'd named Sparkles. Sparkles rarely left the bag that Taylor wore over her shoulders almost all the time. Whenever she didn't have her grungy yellow bag on her shoulders, she'd feel a sense of panic.

Most kids had a security blanket. Taylor had a security backpack with all her most cherished belongings inside. Just in case.

That was the biggest life lesson she'd learned by the time she was six. Have a bag packed, just in case. Be ready to run, just in case. Don't get too attached, just in case.

Another vicious sound erupted from her as she swung at the pink painted wall. The drywall gave way with a crack, and she yanked the hammer head free before smashing it again. Every time she swung, she thought of some other shitty lesson her mother had taught her.

Don't mix beer with the hard stuff, kid.

Keep your shoes by the bed. You never know when we might have to bail.

Don't think of it as taking from someone else, baby girl. Think of it as investing in ourselves.

Taylor hadn't thought about those lessons in a long time, but now she couldn't stop. And she couldn't stop seeing the new image of her now-aged mother in her mind.

She wished she could take it back. She wished she could go back to not knowing where her mother was and what she looked like. But as much as she wished she'd never found out about her mother, the idea of not knowing had no longer been acceptable.

Taylor swung again, and again, but finally her body screamed in protest loudly enough that she could no longer ignore the pain she was causing herself. Her muscles ached, her lungs burned, and her eyes... Her eyes stung from the tears that she hadn't noticed were falling down her face.

She'd been a kid. She should have had a pink room and a bed to sleep in. She should have had security. She shouldn't have had to deal with all the bullshit her mother had dragged her into.

"I waited until you were done this time," Darby said softly from behind Taylor.

Taylor turned and saw her friends standing inside the door, both looking concerned. She wished she could tell them not to worry, but words seemed to fail her. She opened her mouth, but a choking sob came out.

"Oh, no," Darby said and rushed forward.

The realization that not only was she crying but she'd been caught crying caused Taylor's anger at her mother to flare again. She'd felt this breakdown coming half the night and most of the morning. That was why she'd avoided morning coffee at the cove for the second day in a row. "I hate her," she finally managed to say through clenched teeth. "I hate her so much."

"I know," Darby whispered as she leaned in to hug Taylor.

"No," Taylor protested, pulling away. "I'm gross."

"You always are," Darby said.

Taylor didn't want to laugh, but she chuckled softly. She

shook her head, and Darby lowered her outstretched arms, but the sorrow on her face didn't lessen.

"You okay, boo?" she asked softly.

"I will be," Taylor said, though she wasn't sure she believed that. She'd opened Pandora's Box and unleashed all kinds of emotional hell that she was already starting to realize she hadn't been prepared to handle. She had known she wasn't ready, but she'd done it anyway.

Though it was usually Jade or Darby who jumped in with both feet, this time it was Taylor. And she was getting a harsh reminder why she tended to overanalyze everything before making a decision.

Jade brushed a strand of sweaty hair from Taylor's forehead. "You need a drink."

"I need a sanity check," Taylor countered. Standing back, she looked at the destruction she'd caused in the room. A good chunk of the wall had been knocked out. Her anger might be eating her alive right now, but it was certainly making her productive.

"Sit," Jade instructed even though there wasn't a single piece of furniture in the room.

Taylor crossed the room to where she hadn't started unleashing her fury and slid down the wall until her butt hit the floor. She accepted the drink Jade held out, sipping on the straw until the tang of cherry soda hit her tongue.

"We shouldn't have let you leave last night," Jade said.

Taylor shrugged. "I had to go home sometime."

"But you still needed us," Darby said.

Taylor sucked on the straw, finishing her drink before panting a few times. "I needed to be alone."

"But you *aren't* alone," Jade said in her sweet maternal tone. "We're right here, ready to help you."

While Taylor appreciated Jade's words, she knew, and she was certain they knew, they were empty. "There's nothing you can do."

"We can support you," Jade said.

Darby nudged Taylor with the tip of her bright-red patent-leather shoe. "We're not going to let you do that *I'm a loner* thing you love so much."

Taylor smirked. "I am a loner."

"Not anymore," Jade said. Though she was in tan linen shorts that wouldn't do much to protect her skin from debris, she sat on the floor next to Taylor.

Taylor frowned. "What have I told you guys about coming into the houses during demo?"

"Bring tequila," Darby offered.

"What else?" Taylor asked instead of letting herself get distracted by the joke.

"Dress accordingly," Darby mumbled.

"Are you dressed accordingly?" Taylor gestured toward Darby's hot pants. "Or are you dressed for date night at the roller rink?"

Darby flipped her hair. "Roller skating is for squares."

Jade snorted. "Whatever. We stopped by because we're worried."

"You still have to dress for being in a construction zone. There are nails and all kinds of shit around here."

Instead of bickering, Jade blinked several times. "Are you done diverting?"

"No," Taylor stated and snagged the drink from Jade's hand. She didn't have to ask. She knew it'd contain some mix of cranberry juice. Jade lived on cranberry juice. She took a big drink and smacked her lips. "Pineapple?"

"Yeah."

"Not bad."

Jade swiped her drink back. "What's going through your head?"

Darby snorted. "Well, that's a loaded question."

Jade shot Darby a warning look, which caused her to frown, but she got the message. Now wasn't the time to tease Taylor. Silence lingered in the room while Taylor debated what, if anything, she should say.

Then, without any further prompting, the words tumbled from her. "I kind of hoped…" She laughed lightly at the tremble in her voice. "I had hoped that maybe she would have her life together. I wanted to think that maybe she'd grown up a little over the years. Prison should have helped her get her head on straight, but…she's a bartender at some dive and living in a shit apartment. She hasn't grown. She hasn't changed. She's probably still the same lame-ass loser she always was."

"Hey, I was a bartender for a long time, and I'm grown up," Darby said but then rolled her eyes. "Okay, I'm not the best example, but just because she's tending bar doesn't mean she isn't walking the line, you know. And the apartment complex may not be as bad as it seems. Like Jade said last night, maybe she's fallen on hard times. She might be working hard to pull herself up."

"Yeah," Taylor said, but in her heart, she didn't believe it. The sense of disappointment she felt was so familiar. She'd always felt this way where her mom was concerned. Even as a child who didn't fully understand what her mother was up to, Taylor had known her mom wasn't a good person. And she'd felt a heavy sense of disappointment all the way down to her young soul.

That was a pretty big burden for a six-year-old to carry, but it was familiar. It was *Mom*. That feeling was Mom. So this fit. This sense that she had confirmed what she'd always known—she was better off without her mom in her life.

"Part of me was still holding on to some hope that maybe…"

"Maybe she'd somehow turned into a mom like we had," Jade said.

Taylor nodded. "Wouldn't it be something if I found her, and we reconnected, and she was just…normal? Wouldn't that be something?" She smiled, but her lips fell quickly. "Look at her. She's…she's not normal."

Once again, there was a heavy silence. "You don't know what she's like," Darby said gently. "You can't know from looking at what she's posted on social media. You can't decide she isn't worthy based on where she works or lives."

"Darby's right," Jade said. "Maybe you should…call her."

Taylor's heart nearly stopped beating at the idea. "Did you find a number for her?"

"No, but the bar where she works has a phone."

The way Taylor's fingers began to tremble was a warning. Fear was filling her chest and making her heart race, sending a surge of adrenaline through her veins. That was a sign. A sign she intended to listen to. She shook her head. "No."

"Okay," Jade said, immediately backing down. "But it's an option."

Taylor nodded. After a few seconds, she dropped her

head back against the wall and closed her eyes. "If I called her, she'd probably just hang up on me."

"Then you'd know what you need to know," Darby said.

That same old sadness and disappointment clouded Taylor's heart. "No. I wouldn't. I still wouldn't know why, and that's what's killing me. Why? Why didn't she come back?" She hated how her voice cracked and the tears bit at her eyes again. She closed her eyes so they couldn't fall. She wouldn't cry again. She'd cried once, and that was all Susan O'Shea was going to get from her. After a long, deep breath, she blew it out and looked up at Darby. "I want answers, and there's only one way to get them. I have to confront her. Face to face. But I just don't think I can. Not yet."

Darby darted concerned eyes to Jade. Jade sighed and nodded. "Well," she said, "you let us know when you're ready. We'll tie that bitch to a chair until you're done with her."

Taylor smiled at the image that filled her mind. "I knew there was a reason we were friends."

Nine p.m. was a little late for a cup of coffee, but Taylor poured one anyway. With the steaming cup of black brew in her hand, she stepped out on the rickety deck of her rental and tore open a packet of cigarettes. Though she had never smoked, she tapped out the first full-flavored cigarette like a pro and struck a match to light it. She didn't inhale—doing so would make her sick—but now and again, she lit one and the wretched scent surrounded her.

The smells of burning tobacco and black coffee reminded her of her grandfather. Though he had never offered any kind of comfort to her, the scents had a way of soothing her. She had learned that by sitting in a diner late one night all by herself. An old man at the table next to hers lit a cigarette and blew into his coffee, and the strangest sense of calm washed over Taylor. She could almost picture her grandfather sitting across from her, slouched in the booth as he bitched about something or other.

The man hadn't been comforting. Not like many would expect. But his presence had been the safest place Taylor had ever known, and every now and then, she needed to be reminded of that feeling.

Sitting in a rocking chair, she looked out over the neighborhood where she'd lived for the last two years. The aroma permeated the air and brought thoughts of her childhood to the forefront of her mind. If her grandfather were sitting there with her now, he'd be making comments about all the plans he had to fix up the place. Plans they both knew he'd never follow through on. But Taylor would have engaged in Grandpa's big talk anyway because that was the type of relationship they had. Their conversations were never deep and often went in circles about things they knew would never happen, but it was conversation. It was company.

As much as Taylor didn't want to admit that her mother had influenced her life choices, Taylor had a tendency to not get too attached to people, places, or things.

People left. Places changed. Things broke or disappeared.

The few people she'd let in—her grandfather and ex-husband—had left in one way or another. She'd been quick to relocate after her divorce—picking a place on the map without much thought. And things—like the tools her ex had taken when he'd disappeared—had been replaced with newer and better models.

Her mother had always told Taylor they didn't live in nice places because nice places were harder to leave. Walking away from a dump was easy. Men came and went because they weren't worth caring about.

Clearly she'd felt the exact same way about having a kid. Everything and everyone was disposable according to the gospel of Susan O'Shea.

So why the hell was Taylor tempting fate by even thinking about her mother?

For the first time in her life, Taylor didn't feel like she had to hide. She had peace. More than that, her life was peaceful. She'd put much of her inner turmoil to rest.

Did she really want to disrupt that? Did she really want to invite her mother in to turn her world upside down? The Susan O'Shea that Taylor remembered was like a hurricane.

Taylor didn't think she could handle that. Not now. Not when she was so settled.

But she wasn't settled. Not really. When she sat like this, in the dark, alone with nothing but a burning cigarette and a cup of coffee to keep her company, part of her always wondered what she could have possibly done to deserve to be abandoned by her own mother. What was wrong with her that her shithead mom didn't think she was good enough to pick up from her extended stay with her grandfather?

She inhaled deeply as the wind blew the cigarette smoke in her direction. A smile tugged at her lips. Yes, the habit was a nasty one, one that she'd lectured her grandfather about plenty of times, but the scent was so comforting.

"Well," she said to his memory, "what do we do now?"

Taylor chuckled, certain she knew exactly what he'd say.

"What do we do?" he'd repeat in that gravely smoked-too-many-packs voice of his. "We pull our heads out of our asses, pick up our feet, and move on down the damn road. There ain't no reason to look back, Taylor. Looking back won't change a damn thing."

Her grandpa had started encouraging her to let go of the idea of her mom coming back for her when she was about eleven. Taylor supposed he knew by then that he'd be raising her until she was grown. He'd either figured out that Susan wasn't coming back, or she'd told him she was washing her hands of her kid.

Taylor wasn't sure of the circumstance that led him to start encouraging her to move on, but he had. And she was thankful for it. If he hadn't, she probably would have held on to some misguided idea that her mom would resurface a changed person, finally ready to be the mom every kid deserved.

Her grandpa had known that would never happen and helped Taylor move on. Even if his means were a little too blunt at times, his heart had been in the right place. And it'd be in the right place if he were still around. He'd tell her to burn that damn folder and never think about her mother again.

Susan was an only child, but her father had no illusions about the type of person she'd been. He had blamed her downfall on drugs, alcohol, and a man named Chuck. Taylor had asked if Chuck was her father, but Grandpa said he didn't know. All he knew was this Chuck person cussed and drank like a sailor. He'd been rebellious and full of himself and had drawn Susan in like the proverbial moth to a flame.

Apparently, Chuck had drawn Susan into the life of schemes that had eventually landed her in prison. According to Grandpa, before she'd turned into a wild teen, Susan had been withdrawn. She'd never quite fit in and hadn't had many friends. She was a nice girl, Grandpa said. Too nice. She'd been gullible and had easily been led astray.

Taylor couldn't imagine her mom as a docile girl. The mom she remembered was a professional liar. She had a loud, infectious laugh that drew people to her. Grandpa might have thought Chuck had been the bad influence, but Taylor could easily imagine the reverse happening. She could see Chuck as the innocent who had been turned to the so-called dark side by Susan's hand.

She'd seen it live and in person plenty of times. Susan had a way of convincing people she was there to help them, to do what was best for them, to propel them forward. And then they'd be supporting her and Taylor before they even knew what was happening. Once they started to catch on that Susan wasn't what she had pretended to be, she'd slink off to find another victim.

Opening the folder, Taylor looked at the photos of her mom that Jade had copied from social media. Despite everything she knew, Taylor's heart lifted a little with hope that her mom had changed. She was working. A real job. Earning her money instead of stealing it. She had an apartment. She wasn't crashing on someone's couch.

Both of those things were huge steps forward from the woman Taylor remembered.

Looking out at the small houses surrounding her, Taylor considered the lessons she'd learned—not only from her mother and grandfather but from her best friends. Jade and

Darby had taught Taylor important lessons about acceptance, personal strength, and trusting the right people. More than that, they had helped her learn that people changed. People grew and overcame their past mistakes. People could do and be better than they'd been in the past.

People deserved second chances. Well, some of them. She wasn't foolish enough to think that was a blanket statement for all the mistakes ever made.

Maybe her mom had been young and foolish and misguided. Maybe she was on the right path now. Maybe there was a chance to have something more than a lifetime of resentment and a childhood of bad memories.

Up until she'd met Jade and Darby, Taylor hadn't wanted more meaningful connections. She hadn't wanted relationships. She hadn't needed something tangible. She hadn't craved having someone she could rely on.

Taylor stared at the cigarette in the ashtray. The ash was long as it slowly burned down to the filter. The coffee no longer released wisps of steam into the air. The scents that reminded her of Grandpa were fading.

All that remained was the fresh air and the understanding that she was probably setting herself up for a fall.

But she had to try.

She had to.

Swiping the screen of her phone, she brought the device to life and opened the group text with her friends.

So, she typed, *who wants to go to Arizona?*

FOUR

A WEEK LATER, when Taylor, Jade, and Darby stepped out of the airport, the heat enveloped them like someone had opened a giant oven door. Taylor winced at the sun, so much brighter than in Virginia. Using her hand to shield her eyes, she raised her gaze toward the crisp, blue sky. Even with her dark glasses, the world seemed too bright.

"Are we in hell?" she muttered.

"No," Darby practically screamed and put her hands up as if to ward off a monster. "I can't. I can't. This heat is inhumane."

Jade chuckled and shook her head, but Taylor barely cast a glance at Darby. Usually her antics would be a welcomed distraction, but every step Taylor took now was one step closer to seeing her mother for the first time in over thirty years. The weight of that was too heavy to be so easily lightened.

Darby put up a second hand. "My face is melting!" Dropping her hands, she heaved a dramatic sigh. "You missed a perfectly good opportunity to comment about using a trowel to put on my makeup."

Taylor smiled slightly. "I'll save my comment for later."

"You're saving your sarcasm? That's not like you." Sagging her shoulders and tilting her head, Darby gave Taylor a sympathetic look. "Are you okay?"

Rather than admit she felt like a herd of elephants were rolling around in her stomach, she nodded. "Just tired from the flight."

Clearly Darby didn't believe her. She once again gave Taylor a sweet smile. However, instead of pressing, Darby commented again on the heat. "I'm not even being dramatic right now. It's too damn hot. How does anyone in this hellhole get breast implants? The damn things would melt."

Taylor checked the receipt for the parking spot number of the rental car and pressed the button on the key fob. A few feet away, a silver SUV chirped and flashed its lights. She pressed the fob again, and the SUV turned itself on. "Let's let the air-conditioner run," she said and pushed another button to pop the back hatch. She and Darby loaded the bags while Jade stared down at her phone, plotting the fastest route to their destination.

They stacked their bags in the back and climbed into the cabin. While Jade pecked away at her phone, Taylor settled in behind the steering wheel and adjusted the cooling fan and the vents. Soon, Jade's phone was telling them how to get to the hotel.

As Taylor drove, Darby complained from the back about the sweat running into so-called unmentionable places, while Jade pointed and commented on the scenery. Despite the distractions, Taylor kept her focus on the robotic GPS voice and the surrounding traffic. Mainly because her stomach was so knotted she could barely swallow let alone think enough to engage in conversation and simultaneously drive.

Finally, she pulled into the hotel parking lot and found a spot near the lobby doors. She frowned at the way the air just above the asphalt shimmered and danced from the rising heat. She'd heard people could cook eggs on the sidewalk in heat like this. Now she believed it. She put the vehicle in park before acknowledging her passengers again—a glance toward Darby in the rearview mirror and a weak smile for Jade.

Ever since stepping off the plane, Taylor had felt a sense of dread. But now reality began to weigh on her.

The last time she'd seen her mom was in a private room at a courthouse. The judge had given them a few minutes to say goodbye before Susan was shipped off to prison.

Most mothers probably would have shed a few tears and imparted some life wisdom before being yanked from her child. Susan O'Shea had complained that she didn't have cigarettes and drinking wasn't allowed. She'd wondered if any men would come see her. And, of course, she told Taylor to take a peek in Grandpa's nightstand drawer. That's where he'd kept extra cash when Susan was growing up. She said if Taylor was lucky, he'd still have a few hundred tucked away in there somewhere.

Her mom had sat there in handcuffs, about to go to prison for theft, and had the audacity to advise her kid where to look for cash to swipe.

Idiot.

Though Taylor wasn't sure who was the bigger idiot—her

mom for landing in prison or herself for tempting fate by seeking out said mother. If Susan had been interested in what her daughter was up to these days, she would have shown up in Chammont Point and asked herself. Or at the very least, she would have called. That was what Taylor should have done.

Rather than flying across the country, she should have picked up the phone and called first. Even now, she was in denial about why she had insisted on flying here instead. She'd told herself that she wanted to see her mother. She wanted to face her. The truth was, she suspected Susan would have told her not to come. Or, if she had invited Taylor for a visit, she would have had time to prepare some facade about who she was and what her life was like now.

Taylor didn't want to see a show. She wanted to see the truth. After all these years, she deserved the truth about who her mother really was. If Susan had advance warning that Taylor was on her way, there was no doubt she'd create one of those fake personalities that she'd seen her mother use so many times.

Taylor followed behind Darby and Jade as they walked into the hotel. As they entered the lobby, a sense of disappointment settled over her. The beige carpet and laminated desk made the place look like a cheap knockoff rather than some kind of rustic resort like she'd imagined. For some reason, the normalcy of the space was a huge letdown. She'd never been to Arizona, but all the movies and television shows she'd watched had her expecting something more...rustic. More Old West-ish. Granted, the hotel was a chain, but it looked like any other hotel in any other city in any other state. The decor wasn't localized. The colors were bland. The decor was...boring. Uniform. Mediocre at best.

Here she was, risking what little inner peace she had left, and she was surrounded by the most mediocre decor she could imagine. Normalcy usually would be comforting for Taylor, but this time...she really would have liked a little something to remind her she was on the verge of changing her life.

"Are you okay?" Darby asked again while Jade checked them into the room she'd reserved.

Taylor tore her gaze away from a little coffee stand in the corner of the lobby and nodded. "I was expecting...more."

"It's not bad," Darby said.

"No," Taylor was quick to say. "It's nice. It's clean and all that, but it's not very..."

"Arizona-y?"

"Yeah," Taylor agreed with a chuckle. "I guess I was expecting to feel like we were walking onto a western movie set or something."

"Me too. But there were wagon wheels outside in the garden. That's pretty cool." Darby slid her sunglasses off and scanned the lobby. "The decor could be more localized, though. Like maybe *one* cactus."

"Exactly." Though Taylor wasn't much for believing in signs, the disappointment in their lodging felt like an omen. The first big letdown in what was likely to be a string of many. So far, their trip to Arizona had been hot, dry, and uninteresting. Granted, they'd only landed an hour prior, but still...the lobby seemed fitting. Nothing spectacular to look at. Nothing exciting or unusual. Just...a plain space for a plain visit.

As always, the most exciting thing in the room was Darby's attire. She'd chosen hot pink capris and a black T-shirt. She was wearing practical black flats, but only because Jade and Taylor had made her wear sensible shoes for the flight. Jade said the last thing any of them needed was Darby breaking her ankles if they had to make an emergency landing and rush out of the plane.

Within a few minutes, they were following Jade to the elevator. Once inside, Darby looked up at the camera. "Can you imagine what they capture on that thing?"

Wincing, Jade shook her head. "I don't want to know."

Darby continued staring. "I bet we could find videos online."

"Don't look," Taylor insisted. "Seriously. Just don't."

"Imagine how many of those videos would make you think twice about touching that railing," Darby said with a smirk.

Jade yanked her hand off the support and stared at it. "Ew."

Taylor laughed lightly, and Darby's smile widened. Once again, her silliness had managed to distract Taylor. She owed her friend a big old margarita for all the effort she was putting into keeping Taylor from sinking into the depression trying to grab hold of her. If not for Darby, Taylor probably would be a complete panic-riddled disaster by now.

Jade was wonderful for support but not great at causing distractions. That was Darby's superpower.

Sure, Taylor was on the verge of panic, but she hadn't succumbed to it. Yet. And that was because Darby always seemed to know when to turn on the class clown act.

The elevator dinged and the doors slid open.

"Okay," Darby sang out as she stepped out into a much more elegant setting than the lobby had presented. The hallway seemed disjointed from the lobby, like the elevator had taken them to another dimension instead of a different floor. The bland decor had been traded for shades of navy, gold, and white that felt like they'd been upgraded to first class. "This is better. Now we're getting somewhere."

"This way," Jade said before leading them to their room. She held the card to the door until a light turned green, and then she pushed the door open. Two queen-sized beds lined one wall and a dresser with a television on top lined the other. To the right was a small bathroom with a shower, sink, and toilet. A rack held four neatly rolled bleached white towels that would likely not stand up to the task of cleaning off all of Darby's makeup. They would be calling for extra towels before morning.

The dark-green carpet did little to make the beige walls feel more welcoming. The upgrades in the hallway had stopped there. This room was definitely outdated.

"Yes," Darby said, marching right to the window where the view was of more buildings. The bright sun reflected off glass and steel, making it even brighter than it'd been outside. The view was cold. Unfeeling. Disconnected. "I always felt like I belonged in the city. I love Chammont Point, don't get me wrong, but this... I live for this kind of setting."

"If that were true," Taylor said as she dropped her duffel bag onto one of the beds, "you would have gone with Noah to LA when he asked."

Darby turned with an eyebrow cocked. Though she and Noah, a successful podcaster, had only dated for six months before he'd landed a show in LA, their relationship had been pretty intense. Even so, Darby turned down his invite to take her with him to California. "I was not going to leave my two best friends for a man. No, thank you. Besides," she said, "our relationship was about to run its course. He was getting clingy."

Jade chuckled but didn't say anything.

"I'm not like you," Darby said to Jade.

With a slack jaw, clearly taken aback, Jade asked, "What does *that* mean?"

"How long were you and Liam dating before he moved in with you? Like five minutes."

Jade didn't dispute the fact that she and Liam jumped into things quickly. Neither seemed to regret it, though. They were perfectly happy. Taylor was happy for them, but she did miss the days when the cove was a man-free zone.

Darby wriggled her fingers and moved her hands around Jade as she dramatically whispered, "You two are so needy."

"Excuse me," Jade stated and planted her hands on her hips.

"We'd barely landed before you were texting him."

Jade gawked at her. "To let him know we'd gotten here safely. It's called being considerate."

"Did you remind him about the delivery?" Taylor asked. "It should be there soon."

"Finn's there," Jade said.

Taylor didn't mean to bristle, but she didn't know Finn and she didn't want him at her project unsupervised. That was a foolish notion, she knew. She should be thankful to him for doing them a favor, but she didn't like the idea of someone she didn't know on her job site.

"It's fine," Jade assured her. "He's done work like that all his life. He knows how to sign for a lumber delivery." Turning her attention back to Darby, she said. "Look, I'm not going to let a good thing slip away. Liam is a sweet, kind—"

"Clingy," Darby said.

"—man," Jade finished as if she hadn't been interrupted.

Taylor tuned them out as she looked at her phone, debating if she should just reschedule the delivery. She hadn't done so because Liam had said he'd handle it. She knew Liam. She trusted him. Finn was an unknown, and Taylor really hated the unknown.

"And we have a strong relationship," Jade continued, disrupting Taylor's debate. "I'm not going to piss that away. In fact…" Jade let her words trail before snapping her mouth shut. A long breath let her friends know she was thinking something but wasn't sure she wanted to say it.

Darby eyed Taylor, and they both grinned.

"In fact, what?" Taylor pressed.

Jade shook her head and focused much more than necessary as she sorted through the contents of her weekender. "Nothing."

"*Nah*. It's something," Darby pressed.

Plopping onto the bed, Taylor stared up at Jade. "Might as well spill it. We're not going to stop pestering until you do."

Jade's cheeks flushed, and she smiled. "I think…"

"You're pregnant," Darby gasped in the dramatic fashion that always seemed to suit her. "Oh my God. Woman with a baby!"

"No," Jade insisted. "Hell, no. My kids are grown. That train has left the station, thank you very much."

"Then what's going on?" Taylor asked.

Jade drew a deep breath. "I'm going to ask him to marry me."

Whoa. Leave it to Jade to jump right in with both damn feet. Sure, Liam was sweet and kind and all that, but marriage? Holy crap. That was a serious commitment. However, it suited Jade and Liam. It really did. The moment they'd started dating, it was like two puzzle pieces falling into place. Taylor didn't know much about romance, but even she knew they were suited for each other.

While Taylor smiled, Darby's face sank as if she'd heard the worst possible news.

"No," she said. "Jade. You can't ask *him* to marry you. He has to ask *you*. That's how it's done."

Blowing out a raspberry, Taylor rolled her eyes. "There are no rules."

"Yes," Darby stated. "There are. There are very strict rules. And *he* has to ask *her*." Putting her hand to her chest, Darby batted her eyes. "He has to set a romantic scene and drop to one knee and pull out the most amazing diamond ring she's ever seen."

Jade giggled. "I'm sure he would if I waited, but I'm not waiting."

Dropping her act, Darby eyed her. "Maybe you should wait a while, Jade. You've had a lot going on. I mean. You're still in mourning."

"Darby's right," Taylor hesitantly agreed. "The last few weeks have been pretty upsetting."

"This isn't because Mom died," Jade said. "Not exactly. Her passing was a reminder to cherish each day. To make the most of every moment we have. I want to do that. As Liam's wife."

Darby sat on the bed next to Taylor. Her bright-red lips twisted into a disgruntled frown. "Fine. But you aren't just going to toss a ring at him. If you're going to break a very good tradition, then we're doing this right."

"We?" Jade asked.

"Hell, yes. *We*. If you're marrying Liam, we're all marrying Liam. I mean, not legally or anything because that would be weird, but close enough. This is our engagement too."

"Oh, boy," Jade muttered. "I'm not sure I like the sound of that."

"Picture it," Darby said waving her hand in front of her face as if seeing a movie play out, "the three of us...four, since we're including Liam—"

"He would probably be there," Jade muttered, causing Taylor to grin.

"The four of us having an intimate dinner in the cove when suddenly Jade throws her napkin aside and whips a ring from her pocket as she drops down on one knee." Darby kneeled to the floor in front of Jade and grabbed her hands, causing them all to laugh. "Liam," she said in a soft yet dramatic way, "you are the filler of my loins."

"Oh shit." Jade giggled.

"The cooker of my vegan meals."

"We're not vegan."

"The paddler of my two-person canoe," Darby said as if Jade hadn't corrected her. "Marry me so we can spend our lives eating veggies and wearing practical clothing made of hemp."

Taylor laughed and shook her head at the way Jade's jaw dropped. Darby situated onto the bed once more and then glanced at Taylor as if to verify her antics had helped.

Once again, her friends had distracted her before her thoughts could become too heavy. "Thank you," she said softly. "Both of you. For coming with me on what is probably going to be the most disastrous trip ever."

Jade eased down next to her. "You don't know that."

"I don't," Taylor agreed. "But I'm not expecting anything else."

"Well, with that attitude..." Darby smiled softly to show she was teasing. "You're going to be okay. No matter what happens, we're going to be right there. And apparently, so is Liam."

Taylor laughed softly. Though she was easily the least sentimental of the trio, she took her friends' hands and squeezed. "Yeah, I will be okay. No matter what happens, I will be okay. I know that. I checked the hours at the bar before we left home. They're open."

"You want to go now?" Jade asked. "We just got here. We don't have to rush."

"I'm not rushing, I'm just... I want to rip off the bandage and get this over with, so let's go rip off some bandages."

She didn't miss the concerned glances her friends shared. Taylor was usually the one telling people to slow down, think things through, be more cautious. She liked to have a plan and an out just in case things didn't go right. Ripping off the bandage wasn't like her. At least not anymore.

She had to admit she'd been reckless in the past. Her grandpa used to tell her that not all her problems could be solved with the swing of a hammer. He hadn't meant that literally. It'd been a reference to her tendency to smash her way through her problems to get to the other side. The proverbial bull in a china shop. That was Taylor. She'd been that way when her grandfather was alive. Things changed. And so did people. She hoped.

She'd rarely questioned herself or her motives until after her failed marriage. That had been the first time Taylor had received a life lesson as a consequence of her own actions. That had been the first time she'd realized she should pause and think things through before jumping.

She'd been reckless in marrying someone she barely knew. That had cost her so much more than a broken heart. She'd lost so much of what she'd had left of her grandfather's belongings when a judge said if she couldn't prove she owned the tools her husband had taken, she couldn't get them back.

How the hell was she supposed to prove that hammers and saws and levels had belonged to the old man who had taught her everything she'd known? She couldn't. And she'd lost them to a no-good jackass who could barely build a box without her telling him how.

Ever since then, she tended to overthink rather than react. Darby liked to tease her for that, but Taylor had learned a hard lesson, and she'd learned it well. However, right now, overthinking seemed like a death knell. Overthinking would put her on a plane headed back east.

No. She needed to find her mother, and she needed to do it before common sense kicked in and she abandoned the idea altogether.

With a newfound resolve, she pushed herself to her feet. "We're not waiting. We're doing this now. *Right* now."

As soon as Taylor walked into Sunkissed Bar and Grill, her eyes focused on the area along the back wall where bottles of liquor were lined in front of a dingy mirror. The wall beneath the bar top was scuffed and scratched from years of people kicking at it. The chairs lining the bar weren't in much better shape. Several had missing support bars between the legs. That could be a hazard and should have been repaired.

Taylor nearly laughed at her observations. She was there to see her long-lost mother, not do a building inspection. She glanced around the bar area again, but there was no one there. No bartender. Or, to be more specific, no Susan O'Shea.

The amount of relief that settled over Taylor should have been a warning sign. That feeling should have told her, without a doubt, she knew that she shouldn't be here. She should leave the past alone. Like her grandfather would have told her.

If the past wanted her, the past would have found her. *The past* being her mother.

However, her mother hadn't tried to find her as far as Taylor knew. She wasn't impossible to find. She hadn't changed her last name. She hadn't been married long enough to bother with an official change. She'd been Taylor O'Shea from the day she'd been born. Until her grandfather died four years prior, she'd lived in the same town where her mom had grown up. A dinky speck on the map of northeastern Virginia.

She could have been found if someone—*anyone*—had tried to find her.

"Have a seat wherever you want," someone called from the other side of the restaurant.

The gravelly voice raked over Taylor and drew the breath from her lungs. The world seemed to jerk to a stop, making her sway on her feet. If someone—she wasn't sure who—hadn't put a hand to her lower back, she probably would have toppled over. Taylor closed her eyes and swallowed down the acidic bile that rose in her throat.

Like her grandfather, Taylor's mother had a distinct rasp to her voice. A sound that had been unforgettable to Taylor.

"We're a little understaffed today," Susan said, "but I'll get to you in a few."

Taylor looked in the direction of the voice. A woman with her black hair pulled into a messy bun at the nape of her neck skillfully carried four plates across the dining room. Her skin was darker than Taylor remembered, but she supposed living in Arizona could tan even the palest flesh.

Susan walked with the same natural confidence that Taylor remembered. When she was younger, before she'd started to realize her mom was a con artist, she'd pictured her as a beauty queen walking stages and winning trophies for being so pretty. That fantasy went away when she realized that not all moms smelled like cigarettes and whiskey and stole from other people.

"That's her," Darby whispered.

Though she tried to respond, Taylor couldn't find her voice. The words wouldn't form. She had come here for this very purpose, to see her mother in person, but actually seeing the woman had shaken her to the core. Of all the times that she imagined seeing her mom again, Taylor never thought the reality would rob her of her senses.

Jade seemed to realize Taylor was frozen and nudged her toward an empty table. "Come on."

Taylor's feet refused to move until Jade pushed her again and a bit harder. Finally, she stumbled forward and landed hard in a booth. Jade bumped her until she scooted over.

"Breathe," Jade whispered and rubbed Taylor's back as if she were trying to get the blood flowing.

"I can't," Taylor whispered in return. "Let me out."

"No," Jade insisted. "You don't have to tell her who you are. You don't have to say anything. Just...get a better look at her."

"I don't need a better look," Taylor stated harshly.

"Shh," Darby hissed. "Here she comes."

Before Taylor could respond, Susan slid a stack of menus onto the table. "Evening, ladies."

Taylor didn't want to look, but she couldn't stop herself. Her eyes were pulled in the direction of the woman standing at their table, and once again the world seemed to stop spinning. As soon as their gazes locked, Susan's smile faltered, and Taylor was certain she'd been recognized. However, in the blink of an eye, the bright grin of a happy waitress returned.

"Can I get you something to drink?" Susan asked, pen to paper and ready to jot down their orders.

Taylor parted her lips but couldn't speak. In that instant, when her eyes met her mother's, her heart nearly stopped beating. All the years seemed to fade away, and she felt like a little kid being told to lie. She felt like what she was doing was wrong. She shouldn't be in that place, doing that thing. She knew better. But there she was, looking up at her mom, waiting for some kind of direction from the person who should know what to say and do.

Taylor's throat grew dry. She couldn't speak if she'd wanted to. Not that she did. She didn't know what to say.

Susan's right eyebrow quirked ever so slightly, and Taylor nearly burst into tears. Her grandfather had that same tic. Whenever he was staring Taylor down, waiting for her to confess to something, his brow lifted, and his eyes bore into her soul. Just like Susan was doing.

"I think we need a minute," Darby said.

Susan glanced at Darby and then slowly met Taylor's gaze again. "Take your time," she said and disappeared.

"She knew it was me," Taylor whispered.

"I don't think so," Jade said as she dispersed the menus. "I'm sure she would have said something."

Though Darby opened her menu, she didn't look at the offerings. "I think she might have suspected. She seemed to... hesitate for a second. Like she wasn't sure what to do."

"Well, she didn't say anything, so..." Jade started but seemed to run out of words.

"What's she gonna say? It's not like we're popping in after school. It's been *thirty* years." Taylor sank back in the booth. Suddenly, she didn't have the strength to sit upright. She shouldn't have been in such a rush to get here. She should have taken her time, like Jade had suggested, to get her thoughts together and formulate a plan. Right now, the only thing she knew was that the walls seemed to be closing in on her, and the air, thick with the smell of old grease, was getting too heavy to breathe.

"Which is why I don't think she recognized you," Jade said. "It's been a hell of a long time since she's seen you...*and* you were a child at the time."

"But I look just like her, damn it." Taylor recalled the

photos in her grandfather's house and how much the generations of women resembled each other. Grandmother, daughter, and granddaughter had far too many shared features for her mom to dismiss so easily. She had to have known she was looking at her daughter.

Susan probably had the same tidal wave of dread wash over her that Taylor had been feeling since walking into the dive. She probably was somewhere right now wondering what the hell Taylor was thinking. Because that was exactly what Taylor was wondering herself. What had she been thinking by coming here? What had she been thinking by stirring up the pot?

This was going to be a disaster. Everything inside her was screaming at her to run and never look back.

Taylor gazed down at the menu. Seeing how upset Jade was at losing her mother had caused some kind of remorse to stir in Taylor's mind. She'd had some crazy urge to reconnect with her mom, but it had been based on emotion, not logic. Logic was screaming at her what a huge mistake she'd made.

"This was a terrible idea," Taylor said. She skimmed the dining room, but Susan was nowhere to be seen. "Let me out."

"No," Jade said. "Look. We came here to pull off the bandage, right? That's what you said."

"I wasn't thinking."

Darby eased her menu down. "If you get it over with—"

"No," Taylor insisted more harshly. "This was stupid. She knows it's me, and she doesn't care."

"You have a right to know," Jade reminded her. "You need to know so you can let go of the hurt you've been burying."

A burning at the back of Taylor's eyes was a warning. She

needed to leave. She needed to go before the anger that had been building in her for thirty years erupted in the middle of a rundown diner. She didn't want a fight, but a fight was brewing. The tension in her chest was getting too heavy, too tight, and the only way to release it was to scream.

But making a scene in the middle of a restaurant was not on Taylor's agenda. She wasn't one for public displays, but she sensed that if she looked that woman in the eye one more time, the cork would pop, and everything she'd been bottling up since she was a child would come spewing out.

That wasn't how she wanted this to play out. She didn't know what she wanted, but it definitely wasn't embarrassing herself with a dramatic show in front of Susan's customers... or in front of Taylor's friends.

She might not have much going for her, but she did have some pride. She did have a little dignity, and she'd be damned if she lost that to her mother too. She'd lost too much to her mother. Her innocence, her childhood, the comfort she should have had as a kid... Susan had taken all of those things away from her daughter. Taylor wouldn't allow her to take anything else.

Panic swelled in her chest like a balloon.

"Did y'all decide what you want?" someone with a sweet Southern drawl asked.

Taylor looked up at the waitress. A different waitress. "Where's Susan?" Taylor asked.

The woman gave a nonchalant shrug. "Said something came up. She had to run some errands or something. She'll be back later. Until then... Do you know what you want?"

Taylor looked from Jade to Darby before scoffing with disbelief. She'd run away. Her mother had recognized her and run away. Why hadn't Taylor seen that coming? And why the hell did it feel like yet another knife cutting through her heart.

Abandonment was something she did her best to never set herself up for, but the sense washing over her certainly felt like that. She'd been abandoned by her mother once again. This time, Taylor had set the ball in motion. This time, Taylor had asked for it.

She bumped into Jade until she moved out of the way. Rising, she said, "You guys stay for dinner. I'm going to get some air."

She ignored the pleas of her friends as she walked out of the bar into the glare of the early evening. The heat pressed down on her like a blanket, and she wanted to kick it off. She wanted to run and be free of this mess she'd created.

Once she was across the parking lot, she glanced back, half expecting her mother to be there in the doorway. But the only ones slipping from the restaurant were Darby and Jade with those concerned looks on their faces that always made Taylor's skin itch.

Taylor gave a dry laugh. Even if her mother hadn't run away, she wouldn't chase her. Her mother wouldn't ever chase anyone. Taylor knew that because one of those wonderful life lessons Susan had imparted is that there wasn't anyone in the world worth chasing.

"If someone wants to leave, baby girl, you gotta let 'em go. Don't beg. Don't plead. Just hold your head up and let 'em go."

That's what she'd said almost every time they'd disappeared in the night. As Taylor sat in the back of the rusty car, clinging to her bag, the words sank in.

Don't chase anyone.

So why was she here?

Standing on the sidewalk, she looked left and then right but didn't know which direction to go. There was nowhere to go. She didn't know this place. She didn't belong in this place.

She was chasing someone who didn't want to be chased. She wasn't begging or pleading, but she was chasing.

And something deep inside told her she should have known better.

FIVE

TAYLOR WAS ALREADY SLEEP DEPRIVED. She hadn't slept well for days. Not since she'd made the decision to find her mother. Now every time she closed her eyes, she saw that crappy diner and Susan looking at her with suspicion. She could still smell the stale beer in the air and feel the grease that had coated the table. Like so many memories of her mother, those few moments in the diner seemed to be haunting Taylor.

She'd spent most of the night staring at the ceiling, rolling the few minutes she'd spent at the restaurant over and over in her mind. Her mind alternated between kicking herself in the ass for even trying to confront her mother and cursing her mother for running out like the chicken shit she'd always been.

Hitting the road instead of facing the consequences of her actions was such a Susan O'Shea thing to do, that Taylor didn't know why she hadn't seen it coming. She should have had Jade and Darby guard the doors while she slipped inside, because she should have known her mother would rather run with her tail between her legs than face her own daughter.

But maybe she had. Maybe Taylor had known, on some level, that her mom would run. Maybe she'd been counting on it because, despite her insistence that she wanted this, she didn't know if she really did. She didn't know if she was truly prepared to face the past.

Some confrontations, though, she was starting to realize there was no prepping for. No matter how many times she tried to think of what to say to her mother, the thoughts got jumbled. Deep down, there was still a part of that little girl who just wanted her mom to hug her and praise her for doing something right. Taylor hated that part of her. She resented the hell out of that part of her that was still so damn broken.

Despite all those lessons her mother had imparted, Taylor had wanted to believe that her mom would be happy to see her. That she would embrace Taylor and tell her how proud she was that her daughter had broken away from a bad cycle. Taylor had worked so hard and overcome so much to be the successful business person she was now, and part of her just wanted her mother to acknowledge that. She'd like to think her mom would see the value in years of trying and failing and trying again. She wanted her efforts to be seen and validated.

And that made her cringe. That made her feel weak and vulnerable.

Not only because she knew better than to want anything like that from her mom but because Taylor always went back to all those times Susan had called Grandpa a loser for being a lowly construction worker. She thought he could have done more, been better. Her idea, of course, was rather than working for someone else, he had enough skills to swindle unwitting people out of money for projects and disappear long before they realized they'd been taken.

She probably would have expected Taylor to take that approach now. Why would she be proud that Taylor struggled because she was determined to be honest? Why would she be proud that Taylor worked hard to make her money? Susan wouldn't be proud. She'd think Taylor was a fool for having the ability to lie, cheat, and steal, and not take it.

"If you sigh one more time," Darby said sleepily from the other side of the bed, "I'm going to suffocate you with this incredibly uncomfortable pillow."

Taylor smirked before sighing even louder. Rolling onto her side, she smiled when Darby opened one eye to glare at her.

Just enough sunlight streamed between the space in the blackout curtains to illuminate Darby's face. "You look so weird without all your makeup," Taylor said.

"You look so weird," Darby countered. "Period. End of story."

"You're both weird," Jade said as she plopped down on the bed Taylor and Darby had shared. She'd already been up, exercised, and showered.

Taylor knew this because she'd seen Jade tiptoeing around the room. She hadn't said anything to let Jade know she was awake, though. She didn't want her friend to worry any more than she had when they'd returned to the hotel room the night before. An eerie quiet had fallen around them as they'd driven back to the hotel, followed by cautious glances at Taylor as if she might snap.

She hadn't. She'd sat staring out the window, processing what had happened, while Jade and Darby whispered and quietly moved around the room as if to not disturb her thoughts.

Jade gestured toward the table. "I brought up muffins and a few other things from the continental breakfast before all the good stuff was gone, but if you guys hurry up, we can probably find someplace still serving breakfast."

Confused, Taylor looked at the watch on her arm and frowned. It was nearly ten. Apparently, sometime during her tossing and turning, she had actually drifted off and slept through Jade's coming and going. She had thought it was much earlier than ten.

"The bar and grill opens in an hour," she said without an ounce of emotion.

Darby pushed herself up and rubbed her eyes. "Let's prepare ourselves before going back again."

"I'm going alone," Taylor said without giving the idea much thought.

"Taylor," Jade started.

Shaking her head as she sat up, Taylor said. "I should have gone alone the first time. I can't drag you guys into whatever mess I might be making."

"We're already in this mess," Darby pointed out.

"Okay," Taylor said after a few seconds. "I don't want her rejecting me again in front of you guys. And we all know that's what's going to happen."

"No, we don't," Jade offered. "She might actually be thrilled to see you."

"She wasn't," Taylor said. "If she was, she would have said so last night."

"Maybe she didn't recognize you. That is possible."

"She recognized me. I saw it in her eyes. She was horrified that I was there."

Jade tried again. "Maybe she panicked. She didn't know what to do, so she…"

"Ran away like she always does."

"Took a break to get her head together. Maybe she came back and we were already gone."

Taylor didn't counter that suggestion. She didn't believe it, but she didn't counter it. She didn't want to continue this back and forth. "This isn't going to be easy or fun. I don't want you guys to witness that." As she raked her long hair from her face, she frowned. "Or, more to the point, I don't want you to see however I react to that."

Darby tilted her head, and the big bow from the scarf she had wrapped around her head dropped. "We aren't going to judge you, Tay. We came with you to offer our support."

"I know," she muttered. Pushing herself up, she grabbed her bag and headed toward the bathroom. "Dibs on the shower."

Taylor took her time as she showered, mostly because Darby had banged on the bathroom door twice, threatening to barge in if Taylor didn't hurry. As soon as she opened the door, fifteen minutes later, a rush of cool air came into the steamy room, and Darby came with it.

"You are rude," Darby stated and then shoved Taylor out. "I was about two seconds from peeing in a cup."

Taylor laughed as she pushed back against Darby's hand. "Oh, wait, I forgot to wash my hair."

"Out," Darby insisted and pushed harder.

Taylor forced herself to laugh, trying her best to act normal as she walked back into the room, and the scent of coffee hit her. The little pot didn't hold more than a few cups, but she welcomed the scent.

"Why must you torture her?" Jade asked.

"Because it's fun."

"You sound like my boys," she muttered as she picked over some fruit.

Taylor dug in her bag until she found her brush. "That's how we bond."

"Now you definitely sound like my boys."

"Do you want me to call to get a ride to the Sunkissed so you guys can have the rental? I don't mind."

Turning concern-filled eyes to Taylor, Jade said, "I don't think you should go see your mom alone. At least let us wait in the car."

As she dragged bristles through her wet hair, she considered the comment. "I'm not going to let things get ugly, Jade. I don't need that weighing down on me. If things start to get confrontational, I'll leave. I don't want my last memory of her to be a fight. Besides, I need to do this alone. I need time to process all of this without you looking at me like I might fall apart at any second or Darby making a fool out of herself so I don't break down."

"We won't do those things."

Creasing her brow, Taylor eyed her with disbelief. "You two can't help yourselves. Look, I appreciate the support, but—"

"You're not in this alone," Jade stated. "I really wish you'd get it through your head that you aren't alone anymore. We are here. For you. With you. Let us help you."

"You are helping me," Taylor said as she stuffed the brush back into her bag. "But sometimes I need to do things on my own."

"I know that. I understand. I don't think this is one of those times."

"I appreciate your concern. I really do—"

"It isn't concern," Jade said, sitting on the bed next to Taylor's bag. "This is big, Taylor. This isn't a first date or lunch with a potential client. This is…this is confronting your mom for an awful lot of shit after thirty years."

"I'm not going to confront her. I don't need to confront her. I just need to ask her why? Why did she do all those things? Why didn't she come back for me? Why is she so fucked up?"

"I know you want to understand," Jade whispered, "but do you think she'll have any answers?"

"I don't know. But I have to ask. Last chance. Do you want the car?"

Jade shook her head. Clearly she wanted to say more, but she bit back her words. "No. We'll hang out by the pool, waiting for you."

"Stay out of the sun," Taylor warned. "You'll be a lobster in a matter of minutes."

Jade scrunched her nose. She might dole out the advice, but she never cared to receive it.

Taylor stuffed her brush back into the bag and snagged the keys off the dresser. She stopped at the door and turned around, "Thanks for being here, Jade. I appreciate it." With that, she headed out, knowing Jade was right. She was probably never going to get the answers she needed.

Taylor drew a deep breath and held it for several seconds before yanking the door to the restaurant open. As she walked inside, she put her sunglasses to the top of her head so she could scan the dining area, which was empty. For some reason, she had expected to see her mom right where she'd last seen her the night before—waiting tables and offering her customers big, fake smiles.

Though the scent of old grease and stale beer still lingered, the dining room was empty. She didn't spot Susan waiting on tables or wiping away messes. The idea that she would be was foolish. The parking lot had been empty. There were no customers to wait on.

"I thought you'd be back," Susan said from behind the bar at the end of the room.

Taylor's stomach dropped to her feet. That voice was a strange mix of soothing and stress inducing. If Taylor were honest, it always had been. There had been some kind of bond between them. Maybe not the traditional mother and daughter bond, but something that had tied them together. That had been comforting to Taylor as a child. Even if she had realized on some level that her mother wasn't a good person, she'd been her mother. That was an odd thing for such a young child to know.

And even more odd, at least in Taylor's mind, was that she still had that understanding, yet hearing Susan's voice offered some kind of nostalgic comfort.

Turning her attention in that direction, Taylor spotted her mom wiping off the bar top. Like the day before, she was dressed casually in holey jeans and a faded T-shirt. Her long black hair was pulled back, and she wore long earrings that nearly reached her shoulders. She looked like she was there to have a drink or two with her friends rather than work a shift.

Apparently the bar and grill didn't have a dress code or a uniform.

Taylor shook that last judgmental thought from her head. Plenty of places let their staff dress comfortably. That didn't take away from the job Susan was doing. Taylor was looking for reasons to cut her down before giving her a chance. Though, something in her gut told her she wasn't going to need to seek out reasons. She suspected Susan would give her plenty.

"Understaffed again today?" Taylor asked, for lack of anything else to say.

"Just about every day," Susan said. "Hard to find good workers who stick around. I don't mind too much. Makes for nice tips." She gestured to the row of stools on the other side of the bar. "Come on over here and have a seat, Taylor."

Hearing her mother say her name for the first time in so long made Taylor's breath catch. Much like she had the first time she'd seen her mom, Taylor swayed on her feet for a few seconds. This time, however, she didn't have Jade to nudge her forward. She had to dig deep and find that strength herself. Doing so reminded her that she'd been standing on her own most of her life.

She had suspected Susan had recognized her. Now that she had confirmation, the fact that Susan had run out the night before stopped being as offensive. Now it was pathetic. This grown-ass woman had run out on her job rather than look at her daughter.

Looking at her now, Taylor felt some of her decades-old anger slip. Susan O'Shea had always seemed so selfish and uncaring in Taylor's memories. But Taylor had to question now if she was simply scared.

Scared of life. Scared of consequences. Scared of everything.

Taylor rolled her shoulders back as she crossed the dining room. As she sank onto a stool, she stared at Susan, taking in every new line and crease that had been added over the last thirty years. Susan never stopped drying a glass, but she did openly look at her daughter in return.

After taking several seconds to get a good look at each other, Susan focused on setting the glass aside. "Your grandpa still alive?"

An unexpected surge of pain hit Taylor's heart. Taylor couldn't remember a time when her mother ever seemed to care about anyone else. To have her ask about Grandpa made Taylor feel protective of him, of his memory. She couldn't recall a time when she'd ever felt like that. Grandpa hadn't ever needed anyone to protect him, but Taylor would be damned if she'd let Susan say a bad word about him.

Instead of issuing that warning, Taylor again reminded herself to reign in her knee-jerk reactions. "No," she answered. "Lung cancer. Four years ago."

"I bet he smoked 'til the end, didn't he?"

"Yeah. He did. In fact, the last thing he said before slipping into a coma was that he needed a smoke."

"Old fool," she said and put her towel aside. She tilted her head and smiled softly—the first show of maternal affection she'd had since Taylor had walked in. "You look like my mama."

"We both do," Taylor said softly. "I have her picture in a frame. We all have the same eyes."

Susan skimmed her face, as if looking for confirmation. The space between them was filled with the kind of static electricity that caused hair to stand on end just before a bad storm. Like one strike of lightning was going to cause everything to break.

Taylor sensed it and suspected her mother did as well. The tension was there.

Finally, Susan looked away. "You want a drink? It's a bit early, but I sure could use a whiskey." Susan didn't wait for Taylor's response. She filled the glass she'd just finished drying and slid it across the bar. "On the house," she added with a wink.

Taylor stared at the amber liquid. She didn't think it wise to drink. Not because of the hour but because she wanted to keep her wits about her.

"You're right. We do all have the same eyes. In fact, you are the spitting image of me when I was your age," Susan said in a tone that almost sounded wistful.

Taylor met her gaze again. Susan cleared her throat and then swallowed her drink down in one gulp.

Resisting the urge to call her out on the bad habit was almost more than Taylor could handle. As a child, she'd managed to associate the smell of whiskey with her mother's poor choices. Whenever that smell was heavy on her breath, Susan would get big ideas that usually ended with Taylor fake crying in the aisles right before her mom would swoop in and rush her out of the store.

"You didn't come here to stare at me," Susan said after taking another shot of whiskey. "So go on. Get it over with. Tell me what a shitty person I am so we can move on."

Taylor considered the offer. The temptation was strong. If anyone ever deserved to be attacked for previous actions, it was her mother. But then Taylor shook her head. She wasn't great at communication, but even she knew attacking someone wasn't the best strategy to getting answers.

"I didn't come here to fight."

"Then why did you come here?"

Again, Taylor resisted the hateful comment that rushed to the tip of her tongue. She wanted to lash out, but she refused. Susan seemed to be trying to goad her into a fight, and she wasn't going to play into that. If she started a fight, Susan would have a reason to kick her out or send her away. Taylor wasn't going to give her a reason.

"I thought we should meet."

Susan smirked as she looked around. "She thought we should meet," she muttered to no one. There was no one else around. Finally, she looked at Taylor again. "I ain't got no money."

"I don't need your money. I own a business."

Susan stared at her for a few seconds. "I ain't got no place for you to crash."

"I didn't come here for a place to stay."

Shrugging, Susan opened her mouth but didn't seem to know what to say next.

"I didn't come here to ask for anything," Taylor clarified. "I just wanted to meet my mom."

"You mean you just wanted to see if I'm still the loser who went to prison."

"Yeah," Taylor said. "I guess."

The muscles in Susan's jaw flexed. She seemed to be trying to restrain her sarcasm too. Or maybe she was resisting the urge to apologize to her daughter. There was a flash of something that looked sorrowful, but the usual hardness returned quickly.

She forced her chin up a notch so she could peer down her nose at Taylor. "I don't steal anymore. I learned my lesson. But I'm not so great at settling down and sticking in one place too long. Men come and go. Jobs come and go. There's always someplace new to see. So I guess in some ways I am. In other ways, not so much."

"You're an adult. You can do what you want, I suppose," Taylor said.

Susan nodded. "Yeah. I always could."

"And you always did." Damn it. As much as she hadn't wanted to let that slip, she couldn't stop it. Taylor pushed the drink away, causing liquor to slosh over the rim and spill onto the bar. "You never gave a shit about me or the people you hurt. All you ever cared about was what you wanted."

Susan smirked. She'd gotten the angry response she'd seemed to have wanted. In those few words, she probably felt validated somehow. Poor Susan. Here she is working hard to better herself, and she's being attacked. Taylor had given her material to gain sympathy from someone, some fool who had yet to learn what this woman was capable of.

That irked Taylor, and some of her control slipped. She narrowed her eyes. She'd come all this way to get some answers, and her mother couldn't even bother to show an ounce of repentance. Not that she'd expected it. But for some reason, Susan's lack of concern cracked the hard outer shell Taylor had been determined to have.

"Do you even care that you left me damaged?" Taylor asked. "You walked away like I was just another mess someone else could clean up. Do you care how that hurt me?"

Susan looked away, and again, for a moment she looked like she might have an ounce of regret for what she'd done. But then she blinked, and it was gone. She focused on wiping the whiskey from the bar. "Look, I don't know why you came here, Taylor, but this notion that we ought to get to know each other is foolish."

Her mouth went dry. She wasn't surprised her mother felt that way, but she still seemed to be in disbelief that she'd say it. "Why?"

Lifting her gaze, Susan stared for several seconds. "Because we're both doing just fine without the other. I got a job. A place to live. You... Look at you. You're doing fine for yourself. You said you don't need anything from me, which is good. I got nothing to give. And I ain't about to ask you for anything. I don't expect nothing from you. So there's no reason for us to do this family bonding bullshit."

Taylor scoffed, as once again, she felt a bit of pity for her mother. "You know, family doesn't always have to be about what you can get from somebody. Sometimes family simply means having someone around."

"Don't give me that fairytale bullshit. We both know family is way more complicated than that. My father—"

"Took me in when he didn't have to," Taylor stated before Susan got the idea to say one bad thing about the man who had given her so much. "He wasn't charming, he wasn't rich, but he did the right thing, which is more than I can say for you."

She hadn't meant for that bit of resentment to slip, but there it was.

Susan simply smirked. "You ever been told that there's two sides to every story?"

Slowly nodding, Taylor said, "Sure. You want to tell me yours?"

"My mama died when I was twelve. He didn't know how to raise me, but he sure as hell should have known better than to have men coming and going at our house all the damn time."

Taylor held her breath as a shock wave rolled through her, but Susan didn't continue. "Are you saying someone hurt you?" she asked softly.

"No. I'm saying I learned to drink, smoke, and seduce men way too young because my daddy didn't know what the hell he was doing. He had men over all the time, poker games, drinking. And then he was surprised when I fell for one of 'em. He threatened to beat the hell outta the guy, but I was in *love*." She drew out the last word and used a breathy tone to emphasize how ridiculous the notion had been. "I moved in with him, but it didn't last six months before he'd had his fill and kicked me out. I couldn't go home. I didn't want to go home. So I moved in with someone else until I figured out how to be on my own. Never looked back."

"Yeah, you're pretty good at that," Taylor stated.

Susan heaved out a big sigh as she heard what she'd likely known was coming. "I was no kind of mama to you, kid, and I knew it. Letting you live the life he was giving you was the only gift I ever gave you. Don't you sit there and tell me it wasn't enough."

"It wasn't. *Mom*."

Susan leaned back, looked down her nose slightly just like Grandpa used to do when Taylor would challenge him. "One thing you need to know about people," she stated as if she were about to impart some great wisdom, "is that nobody is all good, and nobody is all bad. Yeah, I did stupid things back then. Things I shouldn't have, but I did good things too. Maybe you don't want to see it, maybe you don't understand it, but leaving you with your granddaddy was the best thing I ever did. He sent me pictures of you while I was in prison, you know. Your school pictures and one of you all dressed up pretty for a birthday party. I'd never seen you smile so big, Taylor. I'd never seen you shine so bright. I figured he must have learned from the mistakes he'd made with me. He never bought me dresses or sent me to birthday parties. You looked happy. Happier than I ever was when I was growing up with him. He gave you a life that I never would have been able to give you."

Taylor's eyes burned as tears started to prick them. "You never tried."

"You might think it was selfish of me to not come get you when I got out of prison, but I knew you were better off. Your granddaddy might not have been perfect, but he still could give you more than I could. You had a home and a grownup who could take care of you. It wasn't selfish of me to leave you there."

Taylor started to object. Her grandfather had never been caring or protective. He simply hadn't wanted to be bothered with the trouble. And he hadn't dressed her pretty for parties. Her friend had let her borrow a dress and styled her hair because she didn't want Taylor to stand out at the party. Her grandfather hadn't given a shit about that.

Susan shook her head before Taylor could speak. Grabbing a clean towel, she went back to drying glasses and putting them away. "It would have been selfish of me to take you away. You might not want to see it that way, but somewhere, deep down inside, you know it's true. Your grandpa loved you as much as his stone-cold heart could love anybody. He took care of you. It would have been cruel for me to take that from you."

"It was cruel to leave me there," Taylor spat. "At least I knew how to navigate the fucked-up things you put me through. Look at me"—she gestured toward herself—"I don't even know how to dress like a woman. I don't know how to act like one. I don't even know who the hell I am because I never had anyone to teach me about anything other than how to hammer a fucking nail." Taylor swallowed. "He was an asshole, and you knew that."

Susan slammed down a glass. "He was an asshole who could take care of you a hell of a lot better than I could, Taylor. What the hell does it matter now? You survived. You're all fucking grown up now. Let it go and move on." She waved her hand. "You have a business and some friends who seemed nice enough. You don't need me."

Taylor swallowed. She hated to admit it, but she could see her mother's logic. In a twisted, shitty parent kind of way, Susan was right. Taylor was grown. She didn't need her mother now. She never had. Even so, there was some part of her that couldn't understand why her mother wouldn't at least want to try.

"Don't you think we should at least get to know each other?"

That had come out weak, and Taylor regretted the words that had slipped from her when a sympathetic but clearly fake smile curved Susan's lips. How many times could she reject her daughter before Taylor accepted it?

"Why would we want to do that?" Susan asked softly.

A flash of Jade and the bond she shared with her mother hit Taylor. Disappointment immediately followed. "Sad as it is, you're the only family I have left. Unless you've figured out who my father is," she said with a deliberate jab.

Susan smirked. "No. I don't think I ever even got his name."

Taylor suspected her mom was fully aware of her baby daddy but chose not to share. He probably had no idea he had a kid out there. He probably had been married when Taylor was conceived, and had been none the wiser about the predicament that he'd left Susan in. And Susan probably hadn't considered if he'd even want to know he had a kid.

Once again, Susan proved that she didn't give a shit about anyone but herself. If she didn't want anything to do with her daughter, she could at least give Taylor the opportunity to connect with her father. Wherever—whoever—he might be. This woman was far too shallow to care about that. If Taylor found her father, he might want to confront Susan, and God forbid the woman pay for what she'd done.

Exhaling a long breath, Taylor ground her teeth. This was getting off track and going exactly how she had anticipated, and that was pissing her off. She had hoped she'd been wrong about her mom. Clearly she hadn't.

Susan might have cleaned up her act, at least as far as her

stealing was concerned, but at the end of the day, she was still the carefree, no fucks to give, drifter she'd always been. And it didn't matter who that hurt as long as Susan was happy and free of responsibility.

"Look," Susan said as she stood, "I'm sure you're disappointed and all that, but I'm not mommy material. I never have been. You're an adult now, Taylor. You want a family? Make one. Get married. Have a kid. That's what other people do."

"Maybe I could, if I knew what having a family meant. All I know about family is how to be used and abandoned by my mother."

"Oh, boo-hoo," Susan said sarcastically. "You sound just like your brother."

Taylor's breath rushed from her chest as she jolted. She felt like she'd been yanked out of her body. She was suddenly disconnected from the moment. The bar was a million miles away. Nothing seemed real.

"My *what*?" she finally asked.

With a wave of her hand, Susan dismissed her. "Never mind. I didn't mean to say that."

"Well, you said it," Taylor barked. "I have a brother? Since when? How old is he? *Where* is he?"

"That doesn't matter."

"The hell it doesn't! Tell me!"

Susan clenched her jaw as they stared each other down. Finally, she pulled her phone from her pocket and scrolled for a moment before pulling a pen and pad from her apron. She jotted something down and ripped the page free. Holding it between her pointer and middle fingers, she waited for Taylor to take it.

"This is the last number I had for him. I don't know if it still works or not. We haven't spoken for a while."

Taylor stared at the paper for a few seconds before taking it. Susan's handwriting was much neater than Taylor would have expected. For some reason, she thought it should be messy, barely legible, but the name *Lonnie* was spelled out in happy loops of letters followed by a phone number.

Lonnie. She had a brother named Lonnie. "How old is he?"

Susan clicked her tongue and rolled her eyes back. "Oh, about twenty-three now, I guess." She tilted her head and eyed Taylor with sympathy. "I don't know what you're after, but I don't think you'll find it with him either."

"Why do you say that?" Taylor asked, almost scared of the answer.

"I do know who his daddy is. And Lonnie is just like him. Trouble with a capital T." Susan's shoulders dropped, and she tilted her head. After a few seconds, she smiled softly. The kind of smile a mother might give. It was out of place on Susan's face and made Taylor shift on her feet.

She knew how to handle sarcasm and anger coming from her mom. She wasn't sure how to handle sincerity.

Reaching across the bar, Susan gently brushed a strand of long black hair behind Taylor's ear. "You head on back to wherever you came from, baby girl. You live your life and find a way to be happy on your own. Because there ain't nothing good for you here or with that brother of yours."

"Just like that, huh?" Taylor asked. "Just go away."

"Would you rather I fed you a bunch of bullshit about how I've been longing for the day we would reunite? Maybe tell you how things are going to be different now? They won't be, Taylor. You were better off without me then, and you're better off without me now."

The hurt in Taylor's heart escaped with a hoarse whisper. "Because you *are* selfish."

"If that's what you want to think."

"What else am I supposed to think?"

Susan tilted her head slightly. "That we're both grownups, and we don't have to pretend that blood is some unbreakable bond. You really want me back in your life, kid? After all you went through growing up with me? I haven't changed that much. I still drink. I still like men who don't stick around too long. And I still keep a suitcase in my car just in case I decide it's time to hit the road. What the hell am I supposed to offer to you?"

Taylor shook her head. "Nothing. You don't have anything I want." Slowly standing, she looked at the number in her hand. "Thanks for...nothing," she said because she really couldn't think of a single thing to be thankful for in that moment. Her mom was exactly how she remembered her. Maybe a little calmer, maybe not quite so ready to drag Taylor into trouble, but for the most part, Susan O'Shea hadn't changed.

Taylor started for the door before stopping and turning around. "It doesn't seem like you care much, but maybe someday you'll think back and want to know that I'm going to be okay. Despite you and what you put me through. And I have some really good friends now. They love me even though you screwed me up pretty good. And I'm...I'm happy. In case you care, I'm happy."

She turned toward the door before her mom had a chance to break her heart anymore.

Taylor hadn't wanted to talk about her visit with her mom when she'd returned to the hotel. Her friends had respected that. They always respected that she needed space to wrap her head around things. However, when she'd announced she was going for a hike, they had insisted on going with her.

Taylor was surprised how well Darby was holding up. They'd waited until early evening to go for a hike at a local park, but the heat was still almost unbearable. Darby had kept her complaints to a minimum, and Taylor appreciated that. She had no doubt it was taking great effort on her friend's part.

She'd promised Darby an ice-cold beer somewhere other than the Sunkissed Bar and Grill. If she never saw that place or her mother again, it would be too damn soon.

Ever since she'd left the bar earlier in the day, her mind had been a hurricane. She didn't have a mother worth a damn. She'd known that. But now she had a brother. That still felt like some otherworldly thing that couldn't possibly really exist. Some phenomena that didn't make sense. But it did make sense. Just like Taylor, her mother had an entire life after they were separated. While Taylor had been pushing herself to break generations of bad choices, her mother's life had been prison, rehab, and having another child to abandon.

That meant Taylor still had a shot at the family she'd been missing. She still had a shot at having someone with her blood to call her own. Her mother may not want her, but maybe her brother would.

"I'm going to find him," she stated with more conviction

than she felt. Her mom had been a bit ominous about looking for family with Lonnie, but Taylor had to hope that her brother was more like her and less like their mom. He was young... What was it her mom had said? Twenty-three? So no doubt he had some growing up to do, but Taylor could help with that. Maybe. If he wanted to have a relationship. She couldn't help but think how her life might have been different if she'd had an older sibling looking out for her.

As they came to a stop on the dry desert trail, Taylor took a drink from her water bottle while Jade and Darby cast concerned glances. Though they had waited until later in the day to take the hike, it was still hot. The sun was still bearing down. And the temperature was still unforgiving.

"Maybe," Jade started, "you should think about it some more."

"No," Taylor said as she rolled her shoulders back. "I'm going to find him. Well"—she smiled at Jade—"*you're* going to find him, since you're the one with super scary stalking skills."

Jade didn't seem convinced she should, but she nodded once. "Okay. I'll try."

Looking out over the desert, Taylor filled her lungs with the hot, dry air. As she did, she recalled a time when she and Jade were paddleboarding. Jade was emotionally distraught over her impending divorce and let out the biggest scream Taylor had ever heard.

Back then, Taylor had been concerned her friend was losing her mind, but now, she totally understood. She'd come all this way to meet the woman who had brought her into the world, and the best she got was "I'm not mama material."

She didn't know why she let it cut at her. She had been pretty sure that's exactly how the meeting would go.

Susan wasn't lying. She wasn't mother material. She never had been. But she could have at least tried. There had to have been some part of her, no matter how small, that felt a maternal bond to her daughter.

Rolling her head back, Taylor howled at the sky. She let years of pent-up hurt flow free until the veins in her neck felt like they might burst. In the distance, wild animals joined her as her voice faded.

"She's fine," Darby said as several people turned to stare. "She's...you know...calling out to Ra. He's like the sun god. She worships him."

Jade chuckled as the onlookers hesitantly looked away. "The sun god?"

Darby shrugged. "I could have said she's summoning demons."

"That would be more accurate," Taylor muttered. Dropping down, she sat on a boulder and looked around. "What was I thinking coming here? It was stupid."

"It wasn't," Jade said in that gross maternal way that she used when things were going to crap. "You found out you have a brother, Tay. That's something."

"Yeah," she finally said. "I guess it's something."

She scanned the scenery. Somehow the barren land seemed fitting. The dry air and bland colors seemed to suit her mood.

She told herself she wasn't upset about how things had gone with her mother. She was upset that she'd been foolish enough to come all the way to Arizona to get rejected.

She could have simply called. Like Jade had suggested.

But in her heart, Taylor had known that her mom would have hung up. Then she probably would have disappeared so that Taylor couldn't find her again.

The idea made her laugh wryly. Lesson learned. Before she hopped on a plane and headed to meet this surprise sibling of hers, she'd drop a line first. She wouldn't put herself out there like that again.

Maybe she shouldn't put herself out there at all. Maybe she should take this as a different kind of lesson—a lesson on when to leave well enough alone. Reaching into her pocket, she wrapped her fingers around the slip of paper with her brother's phone number, knowing that wasn't going to be possible.

SIX

THE FOLLOWING MONDAY, Taylor was back to work. After verifying the delivery was complete and nothing was missing from the new inventory, she checked her watch for the third time. Frowning, she pulled her phone out of her pocket with the intent to call the guy she'd hired to help her hang drywall. With his extra set of hands, she could finish covering the wall studs before afternoon. Sure, she could do it herself, but that would take twice as long and be twice as irritating than if she had the help she'd hired. To *help* her.

As she did, a slip of paper fell to the floor. Taylor stared at it, wondering why the hell she'd tucked that back into her pocket. She didn't know why she was carrying that stupid slip of paper with her. She didn't need it. She'd memorized the number before she'd even gotten back to Virginia.

"Just call him," Taylor stated, softly chastising herself.

She bent and scooped up the paper before unfolding it. Though she knew the number by heart, she stared at the keypad as she dialed. Her fingers froze before she could connect. What the hell was she going to say? How was she going to explain who she was?

Susan clearly hadn't meant to tell Taylor she had a brother. Maybe she'd never told Lonnie he had an older sister.

"Just call him," she stated more forcefully and tapped the button to connect.

Her lungs grew tight as she stared at the screen and watched it switch from the number pad to a green circle with a phone, indicating the call was being made. She started to swipe the screen to end the call when a voice came through.

The phone wasn't to her ear, but even so, she heard the deep voice. "Hello?" he asked.

Taylor forgot how to breathe. Shit. She'd called him. She'd actually called him.

"Hello?" he said again.

Forcing herself to swallow, she slowly put the phone to her ear. "Lonnie?" she asked, her voice barely above a cracked whisper.

"No, you got the wrong number."

The heart that had been pounding in Taylor's chest dropped to the darkest pits of her stomach. She'd been hyper-focused as she'd dialed. She hadn't dialed the wrong number. She'd been given the wrong number.

"I'm sorry," she said.

"No problem," the man said then ended the brief exchange.

Taking the phone from her ear, she stared at the screen. Then, just to be sure, she checked her recent calls to verify the number. She had dialed right. She'd called the number Susan said was her last known contact to Lonnie.

Pain seared through Taylor's chest. She should have taken Susan's phone and double checked the number herself. For all she knew, Lonnie didn't even exist. Susan might have been lying to her.

Probably had been lying to her.

"Stupid," Taylor muttered as she crumpled the paper and tossed it aside to be swept up with the rest of the debris on the floor later in the day. Shaking thoughts of Lonnie from her head, she returned her attention to Brad, the slacker who hadn't shown up for work.

She wasn't the least bit surprised when he didn't answer. This was the third and final chance she intended to give Brad to work with her. He had a tendency of showing up late, if he showed up at all. When he did, he always had an excuse for his tardiness. Sure, some of them might have been valid, but she wasn't in the mood for excuses on a good day, and this was *not* a good day.

"Brad," she stated flatly when his voice mail picked up, "it's Taylor. I told you last time, if you were late again not to bother showing up. So don't bother showing up. I'm hiring someone else."

She ended the call and cursed under her breath. She had no patience left for slackers. If Brad didn't want a paying job, she'd find someone who did. Of course, experience told her that was more difficult than her pissy rant was indicating. Finding good help that actually took the job seriously was not easy.

Her grandfather used to complain about the same issue. Home repair and construction was hard work, and too many guys showed up thinking it'd be easy money. Once they realized they had to do math to make things fit or actually take the time to level things out, they lost interest. She'd seen it a hundred times.

Tossing her phone aside, she glared up at the bare boards needing to be covered. She could hang drywall by herself with the assistance of a few strategically placed framing nails. The nails could be placed to hold the board where she needed while she secured it to the studs, but that was a pain in the ass. Although, with her dark mood, she might be able to do the work alone. Anybody she brought in was likely to get their head bitten off for no good reason.

She hadn't slept well since returning from Arizona several days prior. Nothing seemed to ease the cloud hanging over her as she weighed calling her brother, and her irritability seemed to grow with every passing moment. Now that she'd called and confirmed what she'd come to suspect as her shock wore off—the number did not belong to her brother—she had hoped to let it go, but now she was starting to question if Susan had been lying.

The idea that Susan had created some mythical sibling to get Taylor out of her face wasn't out of the realm of possibilities. Taylor wouldn't put creating an imaginary sibling past that woman. She wouldn't put *anything* past that woman.

I called, she texted to Jade and Darby. *Wrong number. Big surprise. Getting to work now. Chat later.*

Taylor didn't exactly say that she didn't want to talk about it, but she hoped that last bit about getting back to work would ward off any attempts at comfort and support. She wasn't in the mood for that right now.

Besides, Jade had been looking for information on Lonnie to give Taylor the chance to decide if she even wanted to contact him. She hadn't had much luck. She'd insisted she just needed more time, but Taylor had to consider that, if he existed, he wasn't on the social media sites where Jade seemed to do her best stalking. Not everyone wanted their lives blasted on the internet.

Taylor sure didn't. If not for Jade and Darby, Taylor wouldn't have her one and only account. They'd set up her page to try to help her drum up business for her home repair company before they'd started flipping houses. She barely checked the site now, and when she did, she rarely posted. She was tagged in photos by her friends, but Taylor didn't have much desire to post her own. Perhaps her brother—if she actually had one—felt the same way.

With her hands on her hips, Taylor debated what other project she could tackle that would be easier and a better use of her time, but in the end, she added a few framing nails into the studs just far enough to support the drywall she needed to hang. Though it wasn't ideal, they offered enough support that she could get to work, and she was able to let her mind wander back to the real issue.

She'd been stupid to listen to Susan. Her mom had likely seen right through Taylor's cool facade and realized that she'd been there on some deep-seated desperate quest to find a familial connection that had died with her grandfather. She'd likely made up that story about Lonnie and his loser father on the fly. Taylor had witnessed her do that far too many times as a child.

By the time she was adding putty to the drywall seams a few hours later, she'd convinced herself that Lonnie O'Shea didn't even exist.

"Hope you're hungry," Jade said walking in, carrying two

bags from La Cocina Mexican Restaurant. "We got you the taco platter."

Darby held up a drink carrier. "And a large cherry soda."

Taylor ran the putty knife one more time over the drywall mud she'd been applying.

"Where's Brad?" Darby asked, spinning slowly.

"He didn't show. Again," Taylor added. "I called and told him not to bother. I can find someone else."

Jade perked up. "Finn can help."

"I'll look around," Taylor said. She didn't want Jade solving her problems. She felt like such a burden already. Jade and Darby had been hovering ever since they'd gotten back to Chammont Point. Actually, they'd been hovering since the day Taylor said she wanted to find Susan.

Every day brought what felt like forced support and encouragement. Taylor appreciated their efforts, but the extra attention was a reminder why she tended to go through things alone. Their extra care just kept reminding her that her life was kind of a big pile of shit at the moment.

The look cast between her friends when Taylor turned to face them let her know this was more than a visit for moral support. Much like when Jade announced they'd found Susan, Taylor's stomach dropped.

"You found him," she whispered, causing her friend to nod. "So he does exist."

Jade's sorrowful face said everything.

Taylor sighed. "He's either dead or in prison."

"He…" Darby started as she pulled their drinks free from the holder. "He's actually in Ohio. Outside of Columbus. He spent a little time in jail, but…he's young and dumb, so…he probably just made a few bad decisions. I'm sure he's learned his lesson."

"What did he do?" Taylor asked as she wiped her hands on a rag.

Jade gave that sad mom look she'd perfected over the years. "He stole from someone."

The cloud looming over her opened up and showered her with disappointment.

Stealing was a trigger for her. Not only because her mom had been a professional thief who had used Taylor to do her dirty work, but because Taylor's ex-husband had made off with her grandfather's tools. Stealing was something Taylor couldn't abide by, so of course her friends wanted to ease into telling her that her little brother had taken after their mom.

"Well," Taylor said flatly, "I guess it's in the genes, right?"

As Darby sorted through the bags containing their lunch, Jade took a folder out of her tote. She held it out and smiled sweetly. "He served his time and has been released. He seems to be getting on his feet from what I could tell."

Taylor looked at her hands again. She was procrastinating. She knew perfectly well that her hands weren't too dirty to take the folder. Her grandfather had taught her how to apply putty like it was an art form, so she rarely got her hands dirty. But she needed one more second to get her head around the fact that her life was about to change once again.

Finally, with no more valid reasons to delay, she took the folder and flipped it open.

There on the first page was a photo of a man. Though Taylor had never seen him before in her life, she recognized everything about him. He had black hair and porcelain skin just like her. Just like their mother.

Taylor hadn't a clue what her biological father looked like, and she never would because she was the spitting image of her mom. And, to judge from the photo, so was this young man.

Taylor swallowed hard as she understood without even reading the words. This was her brother. Half-brother to be specific. Opening her mouth, she tried to state the obvious—she had a brother—but the words stuck like gum on the bottom of a shoe.

"I know he's been in a bit of trouble," Jade said softly. "But he seems to be trying to sort himself out. I think you should be aware that he has a troubled past, but I don't think you should let that stop you from trying to connect with him. Not if it's important to you. If he was raised the way you were, it's only natural he started down that path. He didn't have your grandfather to set him straight."

Taylor acknowledged Jade's comment with a slight nod. She understood what Jade was saying. Taylor shouldn't write him off because he'd got caught stealing. Because, honestly, if it hadn't been for her grandfather, Taylor probably would have had the same issues. She probably would have landed in jail herself.

She couldn't blame Lonnie for doing what Susan had undoubtedly taught him. Hopefully, a stint in jail scared him enough to learn the lessons her mother seemed to struggle with.

"He looks just like you," Darby whispered.

"Yeah," Taylor said back just as quietly. "He does."

Taylor didn't know what she'd been expecting when

she'd asked Jade to dig into what her mother had been up to. But she hadn't even considered that she had a sibling out there somewhere. Though she hated all the emotions that so freely flowed from her friends, Taylor's eyes filled with the sting of tears. "I guess she wasn't lying. I have a brother." Her voice cracked as some strange new reality sank in. "I have a little brother."

Darby cooed softly as she put an arm around Taylor's shoulders. "So. Are we headed to Columbus next?"

Taylor closed the folder and stared at it for several seconds. "I don't know. Seeing my mom again was such a letdown. I want to think about this first. Knowing he has a history of theft is something I'm going to have to consider." She glanced over at her friends. "I really don't want to invite trouble into my life. None of us needs that."

"This isn't about us," Jade said gently.

"Not directly." Taylor tossed the folder onto the counter before walking to the sink. The scents drifting from the containers Darby had unpacked were becoming too much for her to ignore. She hadn't realized how hungry she was until the familiar smells settled over her. She squirted some liquid soap onto her hands. "But we are in a really good place with our business, and I don't want to rock the boat."

"How will meeting your brother rock the boat?"

Turning, Taylor dried her hands on a towel as she said, "Okay. I don't want to rock *my* boat right now. I kind of feel like I dodged a bullet when my mother rejected the idea of having a relationship. Something tells me if we'd set down that path, I would have gotten too distracted by all her bullshit. And trust me, Susan O'Shea is never lacking in bullshit. I don't have to know her to know that. She still had that same old aura about her."

"That doesn't mean Lonnie is the same," Jade offered.

Tossing the towel aside, Taylor nodded. "I know. But before I open the door, I have to weigh how much I'm willing to connect with him if he is. I've worked hard to overcome Mom's influence over me."

"You've done amazing," Darby said.

"Thanks," Taylor said softly. Leaning against the counter, she looked at the containers that just a few moments before had been drawing her in. Suddenly, her stomach felt too twisted around itself to eat. "As much as I want to connect with Lonnie, I don't know him. Being half-siblings doesn't mean a damn thing if you're strangers."

She moved to the food her friends had brought and grabbed the container that had her order written on top. The taco platter was her go-to at La Cocina when she couldn't decide what she wanted. Tacos were her favorite. They always had been. Her grandpa used to tell her if she cooked tacos for dinner one more time, he was going to ban her from his kitchen. That was an empty threat, and she knew it. If she didn't cook dinner—tacos or otherwise—they'd eat fried bologna sandwiches and chips every night.

A smile tugged at her lips at the memory, but a sense of sadness wasn't far behind. Not only at her loss, but the realization that Lonnie hadn't ever met their grandfather. She had no idea what his life was like, but if it'd been anything like hers before her grandpa took over, the kid hadn't stood a chance.

Taylor shook away the oncoming sense of guilt. She had no

idea what Lonnie's life had been or what kind of family unit he'd had. Susan said she'd known who Lonnie's father was. Maybe Lonnie had a paternal grandfather who had helped him out. Or aunts and uncles. Maybe he'd had cousins and other siblings.

She hoped for his sake that he had someone other than his mother to help him grow. She hoped his life had been easier. Better. Less traumatic.

However, she couldn't quite let go of the fear that it hadn't, and she would be inviting an entire new kind of mess into her life if she reached out to her brother.

"You don't have to decide anything right now," Darby said. "You can sit on it for a while."

"For as long as you need," Jade confirmed.

Taylor offered them a smile. "Yeah. I know." She pulled a piece of cilantro off her taco and sighed with disappointment. She hated cilantro. She hated that she'd let her mom make her feel like such a loser again. She hated that she had a brother and he'd been to jail.

More than all that, she hated feeling so damn indecisive.

Taylor spent the afternoon reading and re-reading the information Jade had gathered on Lonnie. Every time she tried to start a new task at the renovation, she was drawn back to the folder. Not only were there photos pulled from Lonnie's ex's social media, but Jade had found and printed out articles about his arrest.

According to the news stories, Lonnie had disputed the charges, claiming the items he'd pawned belonged to him. However, his ex-girlfriend, the one whose social media Jade had found, was able to produce her receipts for several of the electronics that Lonnie had sold.

Petty theft.

A misdemeanor.

Six months in jail.

Possibly because of a misunderstanding of the ownership. Or possibly because Lonnie O'Shea was a lousy criminal like his mother. *Their* mother.

Finally, fed up with the vicious cycle her thoughts had gotten into, Taylor locked up the house and headed to the cove where Darby and Jade lived. She usually popped in first thing in the morning or after work, but it was the middle of the afternoon. She should be working, but when she found Darby sitting at the table situated between her cabin and Jade's, Darby didn't bat a false eyelash at seeing her. It was almost as if she'd been expecting company.

The three of them often spent quite a bit of time at that little table going over plans for remodels and laughing at each other's stories. Somehow, though this cove wasn't Taylor's home, it had become her safe place. She felt protected here.

"Hey." Darby held up two samples of material, both in different shades of blue. "Which one screams 'buy this damn house'?"

"Robin's egg." Taylor sat across from her. "It's more comforting."

Darby looked between the two samples, then gawked at her friend. "You knew the name of this shade without reading the label. My baby is growing up."

Taylor scrunched up her nose and stuck out her tongue. "Whatever. Where's Jade?"

"On the lake with Liam."

A strange feeling settled over Taylor. Jade had always spent time out on the lake with Liam. They'd always gone and done things together. That was nothing new, so Taylor didn't know why she suddenly felt put out about it. Liam had moved in with Jade. They were a couple now. Jade had other priorities than hanging out in the cove with her friends. Taylor knew that, she understood it, but for some reason, it felt unsettling.

"I miss our little trio sometimes," she said without thinking.

Darby focused on Taylor. "We're still a trio, Tay. It's a little different now that Jade and Liam are so serious, but it's good, right? It's a good kind of different. Jade deserves to be happy, and Liam makes her happy."

Taylor mentally kicked herself for letting her feelings slip. She rarely let her guard down, but she'd felt irritatingly vulnerable ever since she'd seen her mom. "Yeah, he does, but...things aren't the same now. I guess I just miss how they were."

"Are you okay?" Darby asked, sounding genuinely concerned.

"I don't know. I'm feeling overwhelmed by all this stuff with my brother, I guess."

"Why do you think that is?"

Turning her eyes to Darby, Taylor fought the urge to grin. She was always thrown off when Darby got serious and analytical. Usually, she'd tease Darby for it. Make some sarcastic remark, but today, Taylor simply shrugged. "I want to meet my brother, but what if..."

"What if he's a career criminal like your mom?"

Taylor nodded as she sank back in her chair. "Exactly. I don't think the odds are in my favor here."

"You turned out okay. For the most part," she said with a smirk.

Taylor grinned too. Though Darby was opening the door for their usual rounds of bantering, Taylor couldn't muster up the strength. She was too overwhelmed. Too stressed. Darby's effort was appreciated, but Taylor didn't have the energy to volley sarcasm back at her.

"I guess," was the best she could do.

Darby's smile softened, and she let their bantering fall. "You're a good person," she said sincerely. "Lonnie might be too. You won't know unless you try."

"What if he doesn't like me? I have the personality of a cement block."

"That's not..." Darby stopped. "What does that mean exactly?"

"I'm dull and hard and..."

"Sturdy," Darby offered. "Reliable."

A faint smile touched Taylor's lips. "Rough around the edges."

"Sometimes," Darby agreed, "but those edges can be buffed away with one of those grinding thingies."

Taylor furrowed her brow.

Darby shrugged. "I don't remember what it's called, but you talked about needing one once."

"It doesn't matter what it's called," Taylor said. She knew what Darby had meant and was impressed her friend had actually learned a thing or two about tools, even if she didn't know what to call things.

"Look, if he doesn't like you or if he's some giant loser,

you aren't out anything. But if he turns out to be cool, you'll have a brother. That's worth the risk, don't you think?"

Taylor didn't agree or disagree. Mostly because she was still undecided. If Lonnie turned out to be like Susan, Taylor might never recover from the disappointment. That, in and of itself, was disappointing. Why was she banking so much on her relationship with someone she hadn't even met? Someone she wasn't even sure if she wanted to meet. She'd made a life for herself in Chammont Point. Why couldn't she let that be enough for her?

Something deep in her gut told her she really needed to let that be enough.

When Darby's phone started playing an obnoxiously happy tune, she flipped the screen and stared. Her eyes grew wider as her mouth fell open until she looked like a fish gasping for air.

"Who is it?" Taylor asked.

Darby turned the phone and showed the name. Noah Joplin. Darby's ex.

The two had been peas in a pod for some time, but once Noah was offered a fancy job in California, Darby had ended things with him. She said she couldn't see herself moving across the country for a man. Taylor's respect for Darby grew after that. It would have been just like her friend to do something wildly irresponsible like uprooting her life to follow a man's dreams.

However, even Taylor, in all her practicality, had realized how heartbroken Darby had been over the decision. She'd tried to hide it, but she'd needed several weeks to get back to her peppy self. There were still times when she'd say something about him, and the light would seem to dim in her eyes.

Her eyes weren't dim now. Taylor wasn't quite sure what they were, but she had to bite the inside of her cheek to stop herself from laughing at the face Darby was making.

"Answer it," she told Darby.

"No," Darby whispered as if Noah might hear.

"Find out what he wants."

"No."

The phone continued ringing as Taylor said, "If you don't, you're going to go insane trying to figure out why he called. Just answer."

Darby shook her head but then rolled her shoulders back. She hovered her finger over the screen for several seconds before Taylor reached over and smacked it just enough to force her finger to connect the call.

Lifting her eyes to Taylor, Darby looked horrified for a different reason altogether.

"Hello?" Noah's voice asked through the phone. "Darbs? You there?"

"I'm gonna kill you," Darby whispered before putting the phone to her ear. "Hey...there," she said hesitantly.

With Darby's ear pressed against the phone, Taylor could no longer hear what was being said, but she watched Darby's face. Shock, a slow smile, tears in her eyes, and then she was beaming.

"I miss you too," she said to Noah. "So freakin' much."

That same sense of something unnamed hit Taylor. As Darby had said about Jade—they wanted her to be happy. Taylor wanted Darby to be happy, and seeing the light in her eyes made Taylor realize how unhappy Darby had been since her breakup with Noah.

They hadn't had some dramatic scene, but rather a simple conversation about how they didn't want a relationship that had to span miles. Darby didn't want to uproot herself and move to the West Coast, and Noah didn't want to pass up an opportunity to further his career.

They'd come to a mutual and friendly agreement that it was time to part ways. For some reason, Taylor had assumed Darby was doing okay with that. However, seeing the sparkle in her eyes made Taylor realize how long it'd been missing.

Darby looked at Taylor and gave her a big thumbs up. The way she beamed as she smiled tugged at something in Taylor's chest. The feeling wasn't jealousy, but it was something. Longing perhaps. Not for a romantic relationship. Taylor was not ready to deal with that crap, but something...

Family.

That's what it was. Taylor was missing that sense of belonging. The sense of family. A place to belong. People to call her own.

Like her brother. As she sat watching her friend fill with happiness, she knew she had no choice. She was going to meet her brother.

SEVEN

THE MOMENT TAYLOR heard the ringtone and looked at the screen of her cell phone, her heart did a swan dive into the pit of her stomach. Barely two hours had passed since she'd called the law firm that had represented Lonnie during his trial. She'd left an awkward stuttering message with her name, phone number, and a declaration that she was Lonnie O'Shea's long-lost sister. Could someone please put her in touch with her brother?

And now a call was coming in from that area code. Though it was very possible it was someone from the attorney's office calling to tell her Lonnie didn't want to make contact with her, she knew in her gut it was him calling. They'd shared her message, and he was responding.

As soon as she clicked the little icon on the screen, she'd be talking to her little brother. *Half*-brother.

Suddenly, she completely understood how nervous Darby had been when Noah had called her the previous day. Darby's phone call had worked out, though. By the time she had gotten off the phone, she'd agreed to fly out to LA for a visit so they could "get their fill" of each other.

Taylor had to laugh as she remembered how Darby had batted her eyes and grinned as she'd said that. A booty call. Darby was flying to California for a goddamn booty call. That was just like her.

The phone in Taylor's hand rang again, and she forced her mind off Darby's life and back to her own. She stared at the screen. Read each and every digit. For some reason, they were mesmerizing and held her in a trance until the device rang once more.

"Answer the phone," she muttered to herself. After one more big breath, she tapped the screen with a trembling thumb and then put the device to her ear. "Hello?"

There was silence on the other end of the call. The void in Taylor's chest seemed to grow, as did the fears and doubts. For days she'd worried that he was just like Susan. But maybe he wasn't. Maybe he really had gotten into a bad situation where he'd been manipulated into taking the blame for something he hadn't done. Maybe he was a good guy.

Maybe *he* was better off without her. Maybe he had gotten on his feet and didn't need this distraction from a long-lost sister. What if her sudden appearance in his life sent him spiraling off track again? She'd been so busy making this about her, that she hadn't considered what her brother might be feeling at the unexpected—and uninvited —contact that she'd made.

Taylor closed her eyes, and that all too familiar sense of shame filled her chest. As much as she criticized herself for overthinking, she clearly hadn't thought enough. Or she could have taken one damn minute to consider that maybe Lonnie didn't want to know her.

She was trying to formulate the words to give him an out if he didn't want to speak to her when finally, after what felt like hours, a deep voice said, "Taylor?"

She swallowed hard. Her voice cracked when she spoke. "Yeah."

"It's Lonnie. I...I, um, I was told you were looking for me."

"Hi." She laughed slightly at herself. That was the best she could do? She was talking to her brother for the first time ever, and *that* was the best she could do? She tried to think of something else, but her mind was blank. She turned and stared at a picture of her and her grandpa sitting on the scratched end table next to her ratty sofa. He had been the only family she'd known for so long, and she felt an odd sense that she was betraying him.

That was foolish. But she still felt it.

Closing her eyes, pushing away the surge of guilt she felt for seeking a new family, Taylor forced herself to say. "Is it okay that I called you?"

"Yeah," he said quickly. "It's cool. I mean, I didn't know how to find you so..."

Relief washed away the fear that she'd imposed on him, and her smile widened. "You knew about me?"

"Yeah. Mom talked about you sometimes. You didn't seem real, though." He laughed softly. "You were kind of like the Easter Bunny or something. I knew about you, but I never knew if you really existed."

"Well, I had no idea about you until about two weeks ago. How are you?"

"Uh...I'm...good. I guess. Yeah, I'm good." Another

nervous-sounding chuckle filled the phone. "Talking to you like this is..."

"Strange," she finished.

"Yeah. That's a good word for it," Lonnie said. "How, um... how did you find out about me?"

Taylor looked out the big window in her living room and watched several birds surfing the breeze. "I had this really dumb idea to try to reconnect with Mom."

"Oh," he moaned. "How did that go?"

"Mmm. She told me I was wasting my time because she's still a big-ass loser. So, it went about how I expected, but I was stupid and did it anyway. At one point, she said I sounded like my brother, which was...unexpected."

"I bet. I guess you had no way of knowing about me sooner."

"No, I didn't."

He grew quiet, and suddenly that long-held fear of rejection rose again. She had spent so much of her life fighting that feeling. She'd spent so much time telling herself that she didn't need acceptance and connections or other people. Now that she was older, she knew better. Being on her own all the time, facing all of her battles alone, no longer seemed like the answer. But she wasn't sure reaching out to a brother she'd never met was the answer either. "Are you sure it's okay that I tracked you down?"

"Yeah, it's cool," Lonnie said, and Taylor was able to breathe again.

She silently chastised herself for letting so much of her hopes ride on his answer. If he hadn't wanted to connect with her, he would have ignored her call. He wouldn't have bothered taking the time to respond. Even so, Taylor hadn't realized how scared she was that he wouldn't want to talk to her until he'd confirmed that he wasn't upset she'd reached out to him.

"Whenever she talked about you, I tried to figure out if she was lying. You know? I didn't know why she would lie about that, but I don't think she even knows why she lies. Out of the blue, she'd say stuff like, 'Taylor probably doesn't even think about us.' Or 'Taylor's all grown up by now.' But I never really knew who you were. My sister. That was all I knew, but it was like maybe she made you up or something."

A smile returned to Taylor's lips. "Yeah, I kind of thought she might have made you up until my friend found you."

"How, uh…"

"Newspaper articles," she admitted.

"Figured," he said, barely loud enough for her to hear. "That was the only reason I could think that my attorney called me with your number."

"His law firm was listed in the paper, so… Yeah, I thought he would be able to reach you."

Lonnie was quiet for a few seconds. "I could tell you my ex set me up and lied in court, but that sounds like something Mom would say."

"Kind of," Taylor agreed.

"But it's the truth. She used her credit card, but I paid her back in cash when I could. She had the receipt, but I *had* paid her back. She was just pissed at me because I'd broken up with her after I found out she'd been cheating on me with some guy at her gym. I would have kicked his ass, but he was about three times my size, so that didn't happen."

Taylor laughed. "Good call."

"She got me in trouble out of spite," Lonnie said.

"Sometimes people don't show their true colors until it's too late," Taylor said. Walking outside, she sank into a chair and stared out over her backyard. The small fenced-in area was empty except for a shed where she kept her tools and a lawn mower. The house was a rental, but someday she might buy a place and put in a garden and guestrooms where someone...Lonnie...could visit. "Unfortunately, I've met far too many people like that in my life."

"I'm not like her," he said, and Taylor knew he meant their mother. "I'm not a criminal."

"Okay," was the only thing Taylor could think to say.

Awkward silence lingered on the line for a few seconds before he said, "What about you? Are you like her?"

"God no." Taylor chuckled. "That's definitely my worst nightmare. Clowns and serial killers have nothing on my fear of turning into our mother. I was six when she went to prison. I never saw her again. Until I had the dumb idea to track her down."

"She still in New Mexico?"

"Arizona," Taylor offered.

"Still married?"

A jolt rolled through Taylor, and she had to blink several times. "Mom was married?"

"To some asshole. That was when I left for good. I was sixteen. She didn't try to stop me."

Taylor frowned. "I'm sorry."

"Don't be. I was better off without her."

Sinking back in her chair, Taylor considered that her

mother had told her the same thing. Taylor was better off without her. "She didn't mention a husband, but I didn't ask. We didn't have a very lengthy conversation. She was in a hurry to send me on my way, which wasn't surprising."

"She's never had much interest in motherhood."

Taylor laughed. "No, she hasn't. What about your dad?"

"He's about as worthless as she is. Her husband wasn't worth a shit either, but he did teach me about cars and stuff. I'm a mechanic now. Well, I was before...you know. I don't think they're married anymore. I mean, I'm pretty sure they aren't. Mom isn't the type to stick to one guy for too long."

"Yeah, I remember," Taylor said. She couldn't remember all the men from her childhood. They were a sea of faces where none stood out, likely because they hadn't been around long enough for her to form a real memory of them.

"What about you?" Lonnie asked. "What do you do?"

"I own a business with some friends. We flip houses."

"Cool," he said.

There was an awkward silence for a few heartbeats before Taylor blurted out. "Her dad took me in when she went to prison. He taught me about home repair and construction stuff. I was helping him build houses before I graduated high school. That's really all I know what to do. My friends run the business end of things. I just...I build things."

"That's a good thing to know, though. I mean, I know how to fix cars, but I could never own a shop. I wouldn't know how." Lonnie let out a long breath, like maybe he didn't know what else to say. "So, what was our grandpa like? Was he better than her?"

Taylor debated how to describe her grandpa. He was a good guy, but he wasn't perfect, and Lonnie deserved to know the truth. Besides, their mother had likely told him stories. Taylor had definitely gotten an earful of complaints throughout her handful of years with Susan.

"He drank too much," Taylor said, "smoked too much, and cussed too much, but he made sure I had food and clothes. He tried to be a parent to me, but you know, I was a girl, and he didn't really know what to do with me. I spent a lot of time on building sites hearing things kids shouldn't hear, but I was a good enough carpenter by the time I was sixteen to earn a paycheck. That was nice. Who, um, who raised you, since I doubt it was Mom?"

"I bounced around a lot. I'd spend some time with Mom for a while, but then one of us would get sick of the other's shit." He laughed lightly. "I was usually sick of hers. She drank too much too. Lied a lot. Partied too much. So then I'd crash with my dad or his sister. Sometimes I'd hang out at a friend's house until their parents kicked me out."

Taylor's heart felt heavy. She'd known kids in school who moved from house to house. That kind of insecurity had taken a toll on them. Most of them had ended up in trouble. No one could really blame them. They had no sense of belonging, nowhere to go when things got tough. All they could count on was not knowing. The only people they could trust was themselves. They'd never learned how to rely on anyone, so when things got tough, they didn't know where to turn, and getting into trouble was easy.

She'd seen it too many times. And she couldn't really blame Lonnie if he had fallen into that trap too. Staring out over her backyard, Taylor listened as Lonnie talked more about his childhood, which sounded like it had been far too similar to Taylor's.

He told her that mom had learned her lesson, at least to an extent, when she'd gone to prison. Lonnie didn't remember her ever stealing or using him as a distraction to get away with theft, but he did recognize that she was manipulative. And she tended to go through men like they were disposable. Some of them were rough with him, trying to teach him about life, he said, but Taylor sensed there was more abuse than life lessons there. She didn't ask. She didn't know him well enough to ask.

Again, she recognized that her life could have been worse. Susan going to prison when she did might have been a blessing, one that Taylor had resented for too long. Of all the men who had come and gone, Taylor couldn't remember one ever being abusive toward her. Then again, she'd learned fairly young how beneficial it was to blend into the background and not be seen or heard.

When it was Taylor's turn to catch her brother up, she told him more about their grandfather and what little she knew of any other extended family, which wasn't much. She told him about growing up in a small town and how everyone knew their grandfather and seemed to treat Taylor like she was trouble before they even knew her. She learned how to operate under the watchful eye of everyone around her because having the last name O'Shea seemed to warrant that kind of attention.

Her grandfather never stole or cheated anyone, at least not to Taylor's knowledge, but he wasn't overly kind or nice. Saying he had rough edges was like saying The Grand

Canyon was a crack. People didn't want to get to know him, and he seemed to be okay with that.

She skipped the bit about her failed marriage and jumped right to moving to Chammont Point and making a new life for herself. Warmth filled her chest as she thought about her friends and the life she'd build over the last few years.

She was finally in a good spot. And she was really grateful for that. In some strange way, it felt good to be able to assure him that his big sister was okay. There was life out there after their mother. She suspected he needed to know that.

After about an hour of catching up on their lives, she dared to say, "I was thinking about taking a trip to Ohio soon. So we can actually meet. What do you think?"

"That'd be cool," Lonnie said. The lightness of his voice made him sound sincere.

The lingering fears in her heart faded. He hadn't rejected her. He hadn't told her to get lost like their mother had. He'd welcomed her, and for some reason, that had become so incredibly important to her.

"Yeah," she said around her smile. "I think so too."

The door to Harper's Ice Cream Shop hadn't even closed behind Taylor when she caught Darby's eye. Darby smiled from the table where she'd been sitting, but she didn't squeal and laugh and rush toward her like she couldn't wait to tell her all about her day. Instead, she looked sad. When Taylor had texted Darby and

Jade that she wanted to meet at Harper's for a treat, she figured they'd come to realize she wanted to talk about her brother. She hadn't even had to tell them. They all knew why they were there.

Taylor offered Darby a weak smile in return. She was glad Darby had nabbed a table for them. Customers stood in line from the time Harper's staff opened the doors to the time they closed them again in the evening. The success of Harper's was another one of those curses-slash-blessings Jade had bestowed on several businesses since moving to Chammont Point.

Until last year, Jade had been some big marketing guru in Fairfax. After her husband had ditched her, Jade telecommuted between Chammont Point and her fancy job in the city for a while. During that time, she put a lot of effort into building a smaller marketing one-woman company in her new hometown. Within eight months, she had enough clientele that she decided she no longer wanted to be an executive and quit that job so she could put all her efforts into local small businesses.

Taylor suspected they owed much more of the success of ReDo to Jade's business sense than Taylor's building skills or Darby's decorating. Jade had a way about her, some kind of cosmic karma that seemed to extend to whatever customer she decided to take under her wing. If she headed up a marketing campaign for someone, they were all but guaranteed to succeed.

Taylor didn't take that personally. She knew from years of experience that the power of marketing was what would make or break a business. She was convinced her lack of people skills was the main reason her construction and repair business had failed. The job was easy compared to selling herself to potential customers.

That was something she knew and understood. And that was why she couldn't get rid of this underlying fear that once she did get to Ohio and Lonnie got to know her, that maybe he wouldn't want to know her. Maybe he would also reject her and turn her away.

Taylor pushed that thought away and smiled uneasily as she headed toward Darby. "Thanks for meeting me."

"Of course." Darby jumped to her feet.

Before Taylor knew what was happening, Darby hugged her tight. Taylor used to stiffen and pull away when Darby came at her with these unexpected shows of affection, but over time, she'd gotten more comfortable with Darby's spontaneous hugs. Somewhat.

She laughed lightly and stood still, waiting the moment out—not hugging Darby back, but not trying to slither away. "What the hell is wrong with you, Darbs?"

Darby put her hands to Taylor's shoulders and held her gaze. "You are my friend. I love you. I am proud of you for all the hard work you're doing."

A blush instantly touched Taylor's cheeks, and she gave one of her dismissive smiles. "Have you been day drinking again?"

"No. I want you to know that you are important to me."

"Thanks. You're important to me too, Darby," she said softly. "You don't have to…you know…give me pep talks. I'm fine."

Sinking into her chair, Darby shook her head. "Everyone needs pep talks, including you. You don't have to be strong for us. You know that, right?"

"I know."

Darby looked like she wanted to say more, give more reassurances, but she likely knew that Taylor would run for the door if she kept doling out affection. "Did you text Jade your order? She's in line."

Taylor turned toward the counter, and Jade waved her phone. She was one person away from ordering and had a look of panic on her face. Taylor didn't know why. Nine times out of ten, she got a hot fudge sundae with extra nuts. That was always a safe bet. Even so, she took her phone from her pocket and texted her request to Jade, who was just stepping up to the counter.

Taylor sank into a chair. Sitting there, under Darby's sorrowful stare made Taylor twitch inside. She was better at accepting help and support than she used to be, but like anyone trying to heal and grow, Taylor still had setbacks. Seeing Darby look at her like that made her want to jump up and run.

"How was your day?" Taylor asked instead of telling Darby to stop looking at her like she was an abandoned puppy.

"It was good," Darby said with far too much enthusiasm. "How was yours?"

Taylor nearly laughed. If Darby wasn't trying so hard to make Taylor feel better, she might have. "Fine," Taylor said but without the forced happiness Darby had used. "Did you make flight arrangements to go get laid?"

Darby grinned, a real Darby-esque grin. "Ha! Not yet. I'm going to make him sweat it out a little bit longer. He left me. And I know he left for his career, but he still left me. He's gotta work for it a little bit."

"Hmm," Taylor said, sitting back, happy that the topic wasn't on her. Yet. "You seemed more than happy to give it up when you were on the phone."

"Oh, I am. I miss that man and his—"

"Don't," Taylor stated firmly. She had learned far too much about what Noah Joplin liked in bed when Darby and Noah were dating. She'd had to constantly remind Darby that nobody wanted to know about that stuff.

The truth was that Jade hadn't minded. She had stories of her own. Taylor, the perpetually single one of the group, was the one who hadn't wanted to hear about any of the tricks Darby and Noah had taught each other. Darby wasn't always mindful of appropriate social boundaries, but Taylor was happy to enforce them anyway.

"I was going to say his sweet smile," Darby said.

"Sure," Taylor replied, not believing her.

"Are you really okay?" Darby asked.

Taylor glanced back in time to see Jade heading toward them with their orders. She waited until Jade was at the table before announcing, "I'm going to Ohio. I'm going to meet Lonnie in person."

As she expected, the atmosphere around their table grew tense. Jade slowed her movements as she eased the tray down. Darby widened her eyes and pressed her lips together as she watched Jade, as if waiting for a cue on how to respond. Their actions confirmed in Taylor's mind that they'd already discussed this. They had anticipated this was coming and had debated what they should do when it happened.

"When are you going?" Jade asked. "I'll clear my schedule."

Taylor reached for her sundae. She wasn't sure what she was expecting, but she hadn't expected Jade to offer to drop everything yet again. Her friends had already done that once. They'd all shifted meetings and deadlines around to fly out to Arizona, which had been a complete waste of their time.

"No," she said, poking at her ice cream. "I'm going alone."

"Oh," Darby squeaked out.

Taylor smirked. "Oh?"

"Look," Jade said softly, "that's not a good idea. Especially after how things went with your mom."

Taylor stabbed at the hot fudge drizzled over her chocolate ice cream. "Can we not rehash that again? Please."

"I don't want to rehash anything, Tay, but I don't want you to get your hopes up too high. Not when we know Lonnie…"

"Is a criminal?" Taylor finished. "I talked to him earlier. He said his girlfriend was being vindictive. That she bought that stuff on her credit card, but he paid her back in cash, and when they broke up, she lied."

"According to him," Jade said.

Blowing out a big breath, Taylor let her shoulders sag. "That's possible. There are people out there who do that kind of shit just out of spite."

"Of course there are," Darby said softly. "But…he went to jail. How bad could their breakup have been that she'd let him go to jail if he weren't guilty?"

Taylor shrugged. "People can be real assholes sometimes. You have no idea what someone is capable of until your relationship is falling apart." She didn't mention her ex-husband, but she knew they understood. She didn't know if he'd robbed her blind when he'd left because he felt entitled to her belongings or out of spite because he knew stealing was a trigger for her. She suspected the latter, but the judge let him get away with it.

Why?

Because she didn't have the receipts to prove the tools she'd inherited from her grandfather belonged to her. So she could see how Lonnie could get into trouble for failing to produce a few pieces of paper. But she also understood why her friends were hesitant to trust him. They didn't have a lot of reason *to* trust him. He came from a troubled background. If he were a thief, he would have learned from the best—his own mother.

"He could be trouble," Jade said. "I don't think you should go alone."

"I don't think you should go at all," Darby stated. "At least not until you get to know him better."

"How am I supposed to get to know him if I don't meet him?" Taylor asked with a slight tease in her tone though she was serious.

"Phone calls," Darby stated. "From a far distance. He could be a serial killer for all you know."

"So could you," Taylor stated.

Darby frowned and shoved her spoon into her banana split. "If I were a serial killer, your skin would be hanging on my wall like a trophy by now."

Taylor winced. "Why my skin?"

Darby shrugged. "Why not?"

"That's gross."

Quirking up a dark and perfectly arched eyebrow, Darby said. "Not as gross as driving halfway across the country to meet some strange man who did jail time."

"I didn't meet him on a dating site," Taylor countered. "He's my brother."

"Half-brother," Darby and Jade stated at the same time.

"Look." Jade pushed her ice cream aside and rested her forearms on the table, but only for a second. She instantly grimaced and lifted her arms and took a peek at them. "Why is the tabletop so sticky?"

"When is the last time you saw someone out here cleaning tables?" Taylor asked.

"Fair enough," Jade mumbled. She pulled a bottle of hand sanitizer from her purse and squirted a glop into her palm. As she spread the fruity smelling cleanser over one arm, and then the other, she said, "It's not safe. I know he's your relative, but you don't know him, Taylor. You don't know who his friends are. You don't know what you could be walking into. I don't want you going alone."

"What are you? My mother?"

"I'm your friend," Jade responded without hesitating. "And your safety is important to me."

Taylor stared at her ice cream for a few seconds, watching the colors blend as she slowly stirred the hot fudge into the vanilla soft serve. "I get that. But he went to jail for a misdemeanor. He wasn't an armed robber or a rapist. Even if he's lying about having paid for the stuff that he pawned, that makes him a thief. Not a murderer. There was no mention of a violent history, and my guess is, if his ex had cause to accuse him of abuse of some kind, she would have. I don't think he's violent, guys. I think he screwed up."

"What if he's still a screwup?" Darby asked softly.

Taylor hadn't been able to get that particular *what if* out of her mind ever since deciding to connect with Lonnie. But she also couldn't stop thinking about the stories he'd shared. She may have had a shitty first six years with their mom, but Lonnie had to endure sixteen years of bullshit before he broke free. And his dose of crap wasn't just from his mom. He'd gotten a fairly short stick when it'd come to his father as well.

For the longest time, Taylor had resented her mom for abandoning her, but she was starting to think she should be grateful. Like Susan had said. She wasn't mom material, and Taylor's grandpa had done what he could to give her a stable home. Lonnie didn't seem to have found stability until he left.

"You know," Taylor said thoughtfully, "if it weren't for Grandpa stepping in and raising me, I probably would have ended up in jail at some point too. I probably would be a screwup too. Lonnie never had anybody. But he has me now. I gotta give him a chance, guys. I gotta try."

"Let us go with you," Jade said softly.

Taylor shook her head after a moment of consideration. "No. Not this time, Jade. This time, I'm going to go on my own. I'll check in, though. I'll check in so often you guys will start ignoring my calls."

"Oh, we already do that," Darby muttered and then grinned to show she was teasing.

Taylor laughed lightly. She would usually volley the sarcasm back, but nothing came to mind. Not because she was offended but because she was filled with too many emotions. She never quite knew what to do when her chest got filled with love and appreciation for her friends. That was still a new thing for her. That was the reason she knew she had to try to help Lonnie. If she wrote him off because he got into trouble once, she wouldn't be deserving of the kind of friendship she had with Jade and Darby.

She wouldn't be worthy of the life they'd helped her build. They'd given her a second chance. They'd taught her how to feel and behave like a normal person instead of a traumatized and defensive child. Lonnie deserved that chance too. And Taylor was going to give it to him.

EIGHT

THREE DAYS LATER, Taylor crossed the Ohio state line as rain poured down. She hoped the dark clouds and lingering storms weren't signs of things to come. Her trepidation grew with each mile after that. Finally, she turned off the radio and drove in silence, letting her thoughts race and roll over themselves. She hoped by the time she reached the apartment complex just outside of Columbus where Lonnie lived, she'd have played out all the *what if* scenarios—good and bad—so her mind could rest.

She'd been bouncing around bad horror movie plots ever since Darby had planted an entire garden's worth of bad thoughts. Taylor didn't think her brother would greet her with an ax in hand and a body bag spread across the floor, but she had started to feel an unexpected sense of concern that he might be a murderer. Like Darby had said about a thousand times, nobody ever thinks a relative is a serial killer until they find body parts in the freezer.

But now, after speaking with Lonnie on the phone several

times in the last few days, Taylor thought the most dangerous thing about him was probably his tendency to tell the same jokes over and over. She chalked that flaw up to nerves. She was nervous too, so she didn't blame him.

In fact, she was thankful that repetition seemed to be his worst trait. Hers tended to be getting angry over nothing of consequence and lashing out. There had been plenty of times over the years when she had to apologize to Jade or Darby because she snapped before realizing what hurtful words were about to tumble out of her. She was better now. Much better. She'd learned to slow down and think before lashing out and to take time to consider what other people are going through.

So, she figured with all his bad jokes as evidence, the worst thing her brother could be hiding is a failed career as a stand-up comedian. The prospect that he was a serial killer in disguise didn't really concern her. Not much anyway.

She let that reassure her until her GPS directed her to drive into an increasingly shadier part of a Columbus suburb. The buildings became more and more rundown, and the streets became increasingly covered in graffiti and trash. Her pickup truck wasn't new by any means, but in comparison to the vehicles she was seeing, she was a bit concerned for the safety of her personal property.

Luckily, Lonnie lived in a gated complex. Of course, if other tenants were as free to give out the code as he'd been, that likely didn't mean much. Even so, when she pulled in front and hit the numbers on the box, she felt a bit more at ease watching the gate slide open. The signs posted made it easy for her to find her way to building number four, where she parked in a guest spot and cut her engine and then texted Lonnie to let him know she'd arrived.

Moments later, a twenty-something man in baggy jeans and a white T-shirt came trotting down the stairs. Even if she hadn't been expecting him to come get her, she would have recognized him. He had the same willowy build. They had the same black hair and dark eyes that almost seemed unnatural against their porcelain skin—the same pale skin, though his arms were covered in black tattoos that started on the backs of his hands and disappeared under his T-shirt. Taylor had just one tattoo—a bear claw, because when she'd been younger, her nickname on construction sites was Bear. Apparently she had a pissy enough attitude to be named for it.

As Lonnie neared, Taylor almost laughed. There was little doubt they were siblings. The unfortunate offspring of Susan O'Shea.

As he hopped off the second stair from the bottom and started jogging her way, Taylor smiled. Despite never having seen this man before in her life, warmth filled her chest. An instant connection was born, and that same old feeling of protectiveness prickled in her veins. There were few people in her life that she would stand up and fight for, but before they'd even made eye contact, she knew he was one of them.

This was her brother. Her little brother. The only remaining family she had—unless there were other O'Shea kids who'd been abandoned somewhere along her mother's journey.

Lonnie caught her gaze as he neared her truck and smiled. Even his shy grin was a mirror of Taylor's. They could have been twins.

She pushed her door open and started to climb out. Her feet had barely touched the asphalt before Lonnie swept her up into a bear hug. She wasn't much for hugging, but she wrapped her arms around him and squeezed tight.

Holy shit. She had a brother.

"I can't believe you found me," he said, pulling back. "This is fuckin' wild."

"Yeah," she agreed.

He grabbed her duffle bag from the back of her truck and slung it over his shoulder. She fought the urge to take it back. She never had been one to let others do things for her, mostly because she was used to seeing the darker side of people. Or at least looking for it. It was far too easy for some people to take advantage of others, and she'd had all of that she was willing to take in her lifetime. But this was her brother.

Her freaking brother. She could let the dude carry her bag without fearing he was setting her up for a fall.

She followed Lonnie up a set of open stairs to the second level of the building to a door that had been propped open with a shoe. Glancing around, Taylor assessed the area. She certainly wouldn't have left her door unlocked, even if she were only running down the stairs for a minute. That was brave of him.

However, when he opened the door and stepped aside to let her in, she realized why he hadn't been concerned. His furniture consisted of a rundown, torn, and faded brown sofa and wooden crates that held a small television screen and an old gaming system. Taylor didn't even play video games, and she knew that gray box was outdated.

Lonnie had left the door open because there wasn't

anything to steal. Initially, Taylor was disappointed. This was far too reminiscent of the barely furnished homes of her childhood. The places that Susan took her in and out of before Taylor could find her footing and even start to feel comfortable. Seeing Lonnie living in these conditions made her realize how far reaching their mother's influence was over both of them. Even now.

He smiled sheepishly when she looked his way. "It ain't much, but it's home."

She smiled in return. "And that's something."

"Here," he said in a rushed voice. "I cleared off the bed for you to crash on. I'll take the couch."

He took her bag into the bedroom. Much like the living room, it was mostly empty. Except for a mattress on a frame with no head or footboards that screamed bedbugs and a broken dresser with drawers that didn't look like they'd close even if they weren't overflowing with clothes.

Lonnie's cheeks turned red as he turned to face her. "I've only been here two months, and I've spent most of that at work. I do some odd jobs a few days a week. It's not easy finding steady work when you have a history like mine."

Taylor eased up on her judgment of his apartment. He was trying. He'd messed up, but he was trying. She really needed to stop acting like that wasn't enough. Lonnie hadn't been given the security that Taylor had growing up. Their grandfather had been a rock, even if he'd been a rough one, that Lonnie never had. He'd had Susan, which Taylor knew, wasn't much.

Her brother had hit a rough patch, but that was to be expected when he'd had a childhood like that. The only reason Taylor didn't have a record was because she'd been taken from her mother before her influence could set in. Lonnie hadn't had that opportunity.

Taylor couldn't suppress the urge to try to make things a little better for him. "We can run to the hardware store and get a few things to fix up that dresser. We can make a better TV stand too, if you want."

Lonnie ran his hand over his black hair. "That'd be cool. Thanks." He shrugged. "I can do some stuff like that. I just haven't had a chance."

"That's okay," she reassured him. "I don't mind."

He eased her bag down and stuck his hands in his back pockets as he looked around the room. "So, uh, I don't have much food. But there's a convenience store around the corner if you want some snacks or something."

Again, he shifted and blushed in a way that made Taylor sense he was incredibly embarrassed about his situation. He could have told her not to come. He could have told her that he'd rather she didn't. But he'd eagerly invited her to his home, knowing his living status was something he was ashamed of.

A few years ago, Taylor probably would have looked down her nose at him for that, but having Jade and Darby as her friends had helped her grow and realize everyone was on a journey. Everyone was going somewhere, and a lot of people went through hell to get to that place.

Clearly Lonnie was still finding his footing on his path. Rather than judge him for that, she was determined to offer as much sisterly support as she could.

"Actually, I'm starving. Let's hit the grocery store so I can get some food for the next few days."

The relief on Lonnie's face was clear. Even if he hadn't

said so, he seemed to have feared she'd expect him, as her host, to feed her. Instead, she intended to stock the fridge full of food and let him know he was welcome to eat whatever he wanted.

That's what sisters did. Right?

A strange sense of pride filled her. The same kind of feel-good swelling in her chest she got when she did something that made Darby squeal with delight or Jade dole out those motherly affirmations. She'd never needed that kind of acceptance a few years ago, but since then, she'd learned it was a good thing. Helping people and making them happy was a good thing. And it made her feel good to do it.

If she were a dog, she'd equate the feeling to getting a pat on the head. The idea nearly made her giggle before a warning flare shot up in her mind. She heard Jade's voice in her head questioning everything Taylor was doing, warning her to think first.

She was buying food? She'd been there like ten minutes, and she'd already offered to buy groceries?

As Taylor watched Lonnie walk toward his kitchen, rambling about how they should check to see what he had on hand first, her smile fell.

Her fear of rejection only came second to her fear of being taken advantage of. Both of those things were directly tied to her mother. She didn't need to spend hours with a therapist to know that. She also was aware enough of her reaction to know that Lonnie, more than anyone other than Susan, was likely to trip that trigger for her.

She stood at the counter, doing what she did best—overanalyzing the situation.

Had she just walked into a trap?

As Lonnie grabbed an old receipt and started writing on it, she replayed the events that led up to her offering to buy food. She did that twice before realizing that if anything, she'd jumped before she had thought. That wasn't usually like her, but few things were like her ever since she decided to find her mom.

Taylor really was taking risks—big risks—and that was definitely not the norm for her. There was a reason Darby always thought Taylor was a party pooper. Because she was. Because she thought things through. She hadn't been thinking lately. Not clearly anyway. Lately she'd been impulsive and reckless.

She'd have to be more mindful going forward. But for now, she'd promised to buy the groceries, and she always kept her promises.

"Ready?" Lonnie asked.

Taylor nodded. "Yeah. I'm ready."

Later that evening, Taylor was showing Lonnie how to perfectly season ground chuck for burgers. Over the years, she'd come up with her own seasoning mix that included smoked paprika, brown sugar, and cayenne pepper. And a few other things.

"Okay," he said from where he sat on the countertop. "But where does the blue cheese come in, because, to be honest, that's freaking me out a little bit."

Taylor watched his face as she picked up the small container of crumbled cheese and dumped it into the mixture.

He widened his eyes and stared at the mixing bowl. "Oh. I don't know about this."

She added some chopped red onion with a dramatic flair she'd learned from watching Darby. "You have to add the cheese to the mix so it can melt while the meat is cooking. Then all those juices help keep it moist."

"You realize your invitation to Thanksgiving dinner hinges on how good this burger is, right?" he asked lightly.

Taylor smiled as she mashed the ingredients together. "Why's that?"

"Because I don't know how to make a fuckin' turkey."

She laughed. "You fry it."

Excitement lit his eyes as he broke off into stories about turkey-fry videos he'd seen on the internet. As she cooked their dinner, he pulled up examples and forced her to watch them. When Darby pulled that crap, Taylor refused, saying if she cared enough to watch what people were doing online, she'd visit those sites herself. But she watched with Lonnie. And she even laughed a few times.

When the burgers were done, Taylor set them aside to drain the grease and went to work on toasting buns. After that, she assembled two burgers, ignoring Lonnie's insistence that he really didn't want to try her weird concoction. He said he'd just nuke a frozen pizza pocket and call it good.

Since he didn't have a table, they sat on the lumpy sofa. "One bite," she told him. "If you die, you don't have to eat the rest."

"I might die," he muttered, and lifted the sandwich. "All right. Here goes nothin'."

Taylor didn't know why she cared so much, but she really

wanted him to like her dinner. She wanted that so much she felt ridiculous, but she waited, watching.

Finally, he took a big bite and stared off into the distance as he chewed. After a few seconds, he chuckled around the mouthful. "Holy shit. That's actually really good."

"Right?" she said, smiling so wide her cheeks hurt.

"Damn," he said before taking another bite. A big smile spread across his face, and Taylor's heart filled with pride. Clearly, he liked her burger. "I guess you're cooking Thanksgiving dinner."

She stopped herself right before telling him he should join her and her friends in Chammont Point for the holiday. Thanksgiving was months away. She had no idea if she and Lonnie would be close or not. Or if Jade and Darby would be cool with her inviting someone to their little dinner party that had become tradition.

She'd wait before extending an invite.

When they finished eating, Taylor informed Lonnie of a long-standing rule she had. The cook did not have to clean. He protested, informing her that she'd made the mess, but his protest was in jest. He said he didn't mind cleaning, really, not after having an awesome dinner for the first time in forever. Taylor almost caved in and offered to do the clean up just because she'd loved how they'd gone back and forth about it. Like siblings. Real siblings.

As he cleaned, Taylor stepped out of the apartment and then leaned against the railing while she texted her friends back in Chammont Point. Their group chat had been unusually quiet since she'd left. She appreciated Jade and Darby giving her time and space, but she didn't like that they weren't blowing up her phone like they usually would. She suspected they were just respecting her request to figure things out on her own. That's what she was always telling them to do. Give her space. Let her think. But she didn't like that they weren't checking in on her obsessively. Mostly because that insecure little voice in the back of her mind was starting to question if they were mad at her, upset that she'd come to Ohio without them.

Looking up at the stars starting to shine in the dusk, Taylor chastised herself. She really had to stop falling back on old traumas. Darby and Jade weren't going to reject her. They weren't going to forget about her. And they weren't better off without her.

However, knowing something and believing it at a core level were two vastly different things. She'd mastered the first one, but the second was being a real bitch.

What's up? She typed as a general hello.

Within moments, Darby was responding. *Hey! How's it going?*

Doing okay? Jade asked seconds later.

Taylor spent the next few minutes catching them up through a rapid fire of messages. From the drive to the apartment to her plans to help Lonnie fix his dresser. She was also going to build him a cheap and easy TV stand.

And she read updates on their day and how they were progressing with decorating plans for the property. Then Jade said what Taylor knew was coming.

When will you be home to finish the reno so we can get moving on selling this property?

She hesitated in responding as she prepared herself to type out the next message. *Actually*, she typed. *I think I might be here longer than I'd planned.*

She waited, but neither responded. She imagined they were talking in person before either replied. Rather than wait, she typed out, *Lonnie needs some help, and I want to be here for him. I'll reach out to some of the guys I know to come do some work on the reno while I'm gone. I can give them a to-do list so things aren't at a standstill.*

She waited for what seemed an eternity before giving in and dialing Jade's number. As she suspected, as soon as Jade connected, Darby's voice echoed through the ear piece as well.

"Hey, Tay," Darby cooed.

"Don't worry," Taylor responded. "I can still oversee the project from here."

"We're not worried," Darby said, but Taylor didn't believe her.

"So things are going well?" Jade asked without offering a greeting.

Taylor looked out at the city. "Yeah. I mean…I've only been here a few hours."

"And already you want to extend your stay?" Jade asked.

"We miss you," Darby offered.

Taylor smirked. Jade was giving Taylor the straightforward treatment while Darby sugar-coated what was coming. They didn't want her to stay. They hadn't said as much, but Taylor knew they'd been hesitant for her to meet Lonnie. Their trip to meet Susan had done a bit of a number on Taylor so she appreciated her friends worrying about her.

"He's struggling," Taylor said. "I want to help him out if I can."

"Be careful," Jade said softly. "I know he's your brother, but…"

"But I don't *really* know him," Taylor said. "I know. I'll keep my eyes open."

Taylor sensed, with their silence, they wanted to say more but were hesitant. She didn't blame them. She'd never been one to be open to advice or criticism. She tended to take those things personally, mostly because she'd been on the defensive for so long.

"I'll be careful," Taylor said as a follow-up. "Thanks for being concerned. I appreciate it."

"We love you," Darby said in her singsong voice.

Taylor actually smiled. "I love you guys too."

More silence because she didn't usually make such professions.

"I'll be home soon," she promised and then ended the call.

Though she had ignored the niggling in the back of her mind so many times over the day, the sense grew. Lonnie was her brother, and she wanted to help him. But she wouldn't, not for a moment, forget who their mother was or what she had taught them. Taylor's grandfather had managed to undo a lot of Susan's programming about what was and wasn't socially acceptable, but Taylor had no idea how much of their mother's way of thinking had influenced Lonnie.

As Taylor neared the door, she hesitated at the sound of Lonnie's voice. "I'm a little short," he was saying. A moment later, he added, "C'mon. You know I'm good for it."

The nerves along Taylor's spine suddenly felt like they were on fire. Lines like that sounded far too reminiscent of her childhood. Her mother was always dancing around having to pay someone back.

"My sister popped in unexpectedly," he said, and Taylor clenched her jaw.

Something primal, something raw, roared to life. Fuck that kid if he was going to use her as an excuse. That was a Susan O'Shea move as old as time.

"I backed out of a job so I could spend some time with her," Lonnie explained, "but she'll only be here for a few days, then I'll get back to the work site and get some cash. I just need like ten days. You know I'm good for it."

Another of Taylor's triggers tripped. *I'm good for it.* How many times did her mother say that? More times than Taylor could recall.

"I'll bring half down tomorrow, okay?" Lonnie offered. "And the other half next Friday. As soon as I get paid."

Taylor's anger abated a bit when he offered to pay at least a portion of whatever he owed to whomever. That was more than their mother had ever done.

"I just don't want to work when my sister is here. I want to spend time with her."

That declaration eased the rest of her ruffled feathers.

He was choosing her over making money. Their mother never would have done that.

"Thanks," Lonnie said with clear relief. "I really appreciate it."

Taylor listened for a few more moments just to make sure he was off the phone before walking back into his shitty apartment.

"How are your friends holding up without you?" Lonnie asked.

She shrugged. "Oh, I think they'll get by. So, um, I told

them that I might hang out here a little bit longer than I had initially planned."

Lonnie's face did a weird mix of excitement and dread.

"But I don't want to impose. I mean, I know you have to work, so you don't have to hang out and entertain me. I thought I might take some time to fix a few things up around here. You know, little things. If you want."

His smile eased. "Yeah, that'd be okay. I probably have to get back to work by Monday. I just pick up shifts when I can from a buddy of mine right now, but I don't want him to replace me. I'm looking for something full-time, but with my history."

She nodded to let him know she understood. "Yeah, I get it."

Taylor could see how hard Lonnie was trying. She didn't have to know him to be proud of him for that. Anyone who picked themselves up by their bootstraps and kept on moving deserved some respect.

Grandpa used to say, "You don't kick a man while he's down, and you sure as hell don't kick him when he's trying to get back up."

She was pretty sure the old coot would say that went tenfold when that person was your little brother.

"Listen," she said, "if I'm going to be here for a while, I should give you some money for rent."

His cheeks turned red, and she realized that he probably figured out that she'd overheard him. She never had been very slick. She was too straightforward for that kind of thing.

"You don't have to do that," Lonnie offered.

"I don't mind. In fact…" She rushed around him to the bedroom and hefted her bag onto the bed. She dug through the contents for a moment before pulling out an envelope of cash. She counted out three hundred dollars in fifties. She only carried one credit card, which was for emergencies only, so she'd withdrawn several hundred in cash on her way out of Chammont Point just in case she'd decided to stay at a hotel.

Turning, she stopped, surprised to see him standing in the doorway. She hadn't heard him follow her.

"Here." She held out the cash. "That's still way less than a hotel room would cost me, so it's only fair."

He looked at the money before slowly reaching out to accept it. "Thanks," he said softly.

"You're welcome."

Though a voice in the back of her mind asked what the hell she was doing, she ignored it. She'd been hanging out with Lonnie for hours now. While that wasn't nearly long enough to know someone, she already felt a growing bond with him. She already felt like they were siblings rather than virtual strangers. And, as she'd considered earlier, siblings looked out for each other.

Taylor slipped the envelope back into her bag and clapped her hands together. "Now what?"

Lonnie laughed. "Now I teach you how to play my favorite video game."

"Eww," Taylor muttered as she crinkled her nose. "Video games are gross."

"So is blue cheese, but I tried it."

"Fair enough," she said with a shrug as she followed him to the living room. Dropping onto the couch, she waited for him to get the game started.

As she watched him, she couldn't help but notice the

level of comfort she had with him. She barely knew him, but already she felt like they had a bond. The only other people she'd ever allowed that kind of connection with was Jade and Darby. The realization left her with a mixed bag of emotions. She was glad she felt connected to her brother, but she was terrified too. Connecting with people was a risk Taylor rarely took.

She just hoped he didn't make her regret it.

NINE

WHEN THE TRAIL led into a little meadow, Taylor glanced back and realized Lonnie was lagging behind her. As she waited for him to catch up, she gazed around her at the field of wildflowers. The path they'd been hiking was well-worn, but all around them wilderness was flourishing. She wasn't much for sentimental scenes, but even she could appreciate how beautiful the field was. Bees buzzed as they bounced around the flowers, and birds sang from nearby trees. Outside of the cove, this was probably one of the more serene spots Taylor could remember being.

The scenery at this park was amazing, though she didn't think her brother was appreciating the hike as much as she was. He continually fell behind and swatted at bugs as he sighed.

Despite the heat of the day, he still dressed like a wannabe rocker in ripped jeans and a black T-shirt, and she still dressed like she was ready for the zombie apocalypse in her practical cargo pants and shoes. She smirked thinking of the video game they'd been playing. If the world suddenly turned upside down like it did in the survival game, Lonnie's tough exterior would keep trouble at bay and the Swiss Army knife in her thigh pocket would come in handy for a life hiding in the woods.

They'd last for a while. She had no doubt. They'd both learned how to survive things that somehow seemed much worse than brain-eating corpses.

Once he caught up to her, she started walking again. This outing was her idea, of course. She'd needed some fresh air. Fresh air always helped her see things clearly.

She'd been in Ohio for two days now, and once again, she'd woken up running the last few days over and over in her mind. She was second guessing if Lonnie had somehow tricked her into buying groceries and paying part of his rent. Though they'd enjoyed the time just hanging out, cooking and playing games, she couldn't let go of the doubts in the back of her mind.

She wished Jade and Darby were there so she could hash out the whirlwind going through her mind. This tendency she had to doubt herself frustrated her endlessly. Jade had a way of talking Taylor through these self-destructive cycles.

Taylor could act tough, but underneath her facade, she was still an insecure kid terrified of being used. Trust had never come easy for Taylor, and she was aware of that. Probably *too* aware. And being too aware made her question if she was simply being paranoid when she suspected Lonnie.

She was torn between knowing Lonnie was her brother and reminding herself that the familial bond she had with Susan hadn't meant a damn thing. At least not to her mother. Taylor hated to admit that part of her was still hurt over the rejection she'd faced. That was the same part of her that feared Lonnie would reject her too. She didn't want to feel that way, but she couldn't stop herself.

"You've been here two days now," Lonnie said when he joined her as she watched a bee investigating a daisy. "I've been waiting for you to ask."

She turned to look at him. He glanced away as if embarrassed, causing an uneasy feeling to settle in her chest. "Ask what?"

"About my stint in jail."

With that one sentence, the peace she'd found in their walk shattered. She hated that the calm was being disturbed by Lonnie's heavy topic. This seemed like the kind of place where only good vibes should be allowed, and talking about his criminal past didn't fall into the good vibes category.

But Lonnie was right. Knowing he'd gone to jail weighed on her in ways she didn't want it to. There was a lack of trust there, mostly stemming from the knowledge that he'd stolen from someone. Just like their mother used to do. They had to hash this out so Taylor could let it go and move on.

"What do you want me to ask?" she asked after a few seconds.

Lonnie stuffed his hands in his jean pockets. "I don't know. But you have to have questions. I would if I were you."

Taylor took a deep breath, and said, "You said your ex lied about the theft because you'd broken up. Must have been a bad break up."

He winced. "Yeah. We were seriously dysfunctional."

"You said she'd cheated on you with some jock?"

After twisting his lips around a few times, he nodded but then added, "I kind of cheated on her first."

Taylor cocked a brow as she looked at him. "Kind of? How do you kind of cheat on someone?"

He scoffed. "Okay. I got drunk and screwed around with some chick at a club. I didn't know one of her coworkers was there. She ratted me out."

"So you cheated, and then out of retaliation, your girlfriend cheated with some dude from her gym."

"Yeah. Pretty much."

"How did that lead her to telling big enough lies to get you arrested?" Taylor cocked her head as she eyed him. "That seems pretty over the top, Lonnie."

After a moment, he blew out a long breath. "Well…it wasn't the first time. I may have cheated on her a few times before that, and since she'd forgiven me, she thought I had to forgive her too."

Taylor shook her head. "One of *those* guys, huh? I can screw around, but you can't."

"I screwed up. I admit it. I never thought I'd end up in jail because I can't keep my pants on, though."

"Your attorney really went for the *he said, she said* argument from what I read in the paper."

"That's really all we had. I'd paid her in cash. Can't really prove that."

Taylor nodded. "Yeah. I hope this isn't a habit for you like it was for Mom. She went to prison for it."

Lonnie nodded. "I knew you'd be thinking of that. I think about it too. I did what I could to be better than Mom. I'm not perfect or anything, but the last thing I want is to be like my parents."

Taylor nodded in understanding. "Not being like Mom is a pretty good motivator. It's kept me out of trouble so far."

Lonnie looked down at the ground like he was ashamed. "She didn't use me to steal and shit like that when I was younger, but she lied a lot. She lied so much that I don't think she even knew when she was lying. Twisting reality around was like breathing to her. And she was so good at it that people started questioning themselves."

Taylor exhaled a big breath. "I remember. I still doubt myself all the time." She opted not to share that she was doubting if she'd doled out money by her own volition or if Lonnie had subtly manipulated her into doing so. "That's called gaslighting, by the way. It's a pretty destructive habit. For everyone. By the time someone is done using that tactic, nobody knows the truth anymore."

"Sometimes, though, she was just lying for what she'd say was a good reason. I remember when I was about seven, Mom met this guy at a restaurant. They started talking, and by the time I finished my chicken nuggets, she'd convinced him that we were homeless after running from her abusive husband. She was so convincing that even I started to believe the only reason we were eating in a restaurant was because she'd found twenty bucks in the public restroom while we were using the sinks to bathe. He felt so bad for her, he handed her a hundred-dollar bill on his way out."

Taylor shook her head. "So she was still stealing, in a sense. She was just doing it without stuffing her purse or pockets with goods when nobody was looking."

"I guess," he said. "She might be better by now. I haven't talked to her in a long time."

"I don't think she is," Taylor muttered. "I mean, she's working, but I'd guess if someone took a close look at the books, they'd find things don't quite add up."

Lonnie chuckled. "She'd have everyone convinced they don't know how to add by the time all was said and done."

Taylor started walking again. "Lying is a pretty big trigger for me," she confessed. "Like you can trash talk behind my back, and I'll be like whatever, but if you lie to my face or steal from me...it's over, man."

"I don't think I really have triggers. I guess I didn't let her shit get to me that much. Or maybe I did," he added with a shrug. "I don't know. Self-analysis isn't really my thing."

"Oh, I can give you some of mine. All I ever do is wonder what's wrong with me and why I turned out to be such a hot mess."

Lonnie slowed his stroll as he looked at her. "No way. You seem so confident."

"Well," she said flatly, "I also don't like to show weakness. Gives people a target."

"I'm sorry things sucked so bad for you," Lonnie said. "I mean, things weren't great when I was growing up, but I had other people around to make sure she didn't do anything too messed up. My dad's sister and her husband were strict. They didn't take any crap when I stayed with them. That's probably why I didn't stay with them very long, but they kept me from getting into too much trouble."

"Like going to prison," Taylor said.

"Yeah, like that." After a few seconds of awkward silence, he said, "Thanks for believing me about not stealing. Not many people do."

"Well, I'm your sister," she said quietly. She still felt strange saying that. The words made her stomach flutter in a strange way, like she couldn't quite believe they were true. "I guess it's good your girlfriend left you," she added more lightly, "or the next time you screwed some chick in a club, she might have framed you for murder."

Lonnie laughed. "She was a little bit psycho, so maybe she would have. But…I don't know. I guess I like my women a little wild. Life's more interesting that way."

"I'm the complete opposite. I like calm, steady, predictability. Mom gave me more than enough excitement when I was a kid. I don't want that."

"Boring can be cool," Lonnie said, causing Taylor to chuckle.

Silence fell between them for a few minutes before Taylor asked. "What are your plans, Lonnie? For the future. You can't drift through life and expect to not end up like Mom. You need a plan or goals or something."

He looked around as the trail they were walking started coming closer to the paved lot where Taylor's truck was parked. "I gotta get a solid work record so I can prove myself. I know I screwed up, but I can't let that be what defines me. One stint in jail can't be what my life is about. I just can't seem to get on my feet, though."

The urge to offer him a job bubbled up but lodged in Taylor's throat. That old defense mechanism of hers prevented her from acting without thinking. Her high dose of paranoia played a role too, but mostly the voice that always screamed at her to wait. To think. To see all the angles before acting.

"It'll take time," she said instead. "I think what you need to do is figure out what you want. Where you want to go. Do you want to be a full-time mechanic? Or is there something else you want to do?"

"Being a mechanic is cool. I like it. I'd be okay doing that."

"So, if you want to prove yourself, maybe we should look at the community college."

He blew out a long raspberry. "No way. I'm not college material."

"You don't have to enroll in college. They should have certificates or something so you can prove that you're reliable and trying to do better. You have to show the world you want to do better."

Lonnie ruffled his black hair a few times before looking around. "Maybe. I'll think about it. I'm not making any promises, though."

Taylor stopped at her truck and unlocked the doors. "There are other ways. You have options, but you're going to have to step up and prove yourself. I know that sucks, but you can't expect people to invest in you when you don't give them reason to."

"Yeah. Can we drop this? I don't like feeling like such a loser."

She smirked as she said, "I wasn't trying to make you feel like a loser. I want to help."

"Well, help in some other way," he said lightly.

Taylor stiffened for a moment. She didn't like his dismissal. She wasn't trying to push him. She was trying to help him see that he could do better. But then she reminded herself that he was trying. He had fallen pretty far, and recovering from a bad breakup and a stint in jail couldn't be easy. He was trying, and no matter what their biological relationship was, they didn't know each other that well. She probably was poking where she shouldn't be. Instead of pressing, she asked, "You up for learning how to build a shelf today?"

"What for?" he asked.

"For your living room. Unless the old, ratty crates aesthetic is what you're going for."

He smiled bashfully. "A shelf would be good. I'd like that. And it'd be cool to learn how to build stuff. I know a little, but not like my big sister."

Lonnie cast a glance at her, and she wasn't sure if he was embarrassed by what he'd said or seeking some kind of affirmation. Either way, she wanted to soothe him. She smiled weakly. "Well, you'll never be as smart as your big sister, but I'm sure she can teach you a thing or two."

Lonnie laughed. "Thanks."

"You're welcome," she said and then hopped into the truck.

After stopping by the home repair store, Taylor and Lonnie headed back to his apartment. Once there, she had Lonnie grab several pieces of lumber from the bed of her truck as she dug out her tool kit from the locked storage box.

She'd cut the pieces of wood to size at the store, so all they had to do was start assembling the shelves in his living room.

Three trips later, they had all the boards upstairs, and Taylor was bossing Lonnie around as easily as she did to anyone else. His attempts at helping her level and drill screws into the boards fell somewhere between Darby's fear of getting a splinter and Jade's constant questions about why and how and back to why.

Taylor didn't even realize she was being short with him until he snorted and muttered, "Yes, ma'am," after she'd snapped at him to hold the board higher.

Sighing, she lowered her drill and eyed him. "Sorry. I'm sure you can imagine I don't get taken seriously by a lot of men in my line of work. Being an asshole is kind of mandatory so I don't get walked over. It's just habit now."

"I get it," Lonnie said. "Men suck sometimes."

"Yes, they do," she said as she leaned up on her knees from where she'd been kneeling. Pointing at the bubble in the little window on her level, she explained that he needed to hold the board so that the bubble was centered. Too far to the right or left, and the shelf wouldn't be level.

Though she thought she shouldn't have to explain that to someone Lonnie's age, she did it with as much patience as she could muster. Not everyone had basic building knowledge. Their grandpa had taught her early, but that didn't mean everyone knew those things.

"Okay," she said. "Hold it."

She screwed the board into place continually glancing at the level to make sure he was doing what she'd told him. After the last screw went in, she leaned back, and he removed the level.

"I started building things with Grandpa as soon as I moved in with him. By eleven, I was on site helping him out when some of his crew didn't show up. By sixteen, I was one of the crew. I went to work as soon as I got out of school and spent my summers on site."

"What was he like? Really?" Lonnie asked.

Taylor lifted the next shelf and waited for Lonnie to sit the level on it and hold the board steady. Once it was, she again glanced at the bubble before adding a screw. "He was mean sometimes. He never cared too much about hurt feelings or sugarcoating. But he was honest. Sometimes people can't handle honest."

"Sometimes honest is a nice way to say someone is a bully." He sounded bitter, as if he'd spent too much of his life hearing that excuse.

Taylor added several more screws as she considered his comment. "I wouldn't say he was a bully. I'd say he didn't take shit and didn't hold back when calling people out. Sometimes that person was me, and sometimes I hated him for it, but he was usually right. He wasn't mean, just…"

"Blunt," Lonnie suggested.

"Yeah." Taylor added the last screw and stood. The shelf was only three feet wide and two shelves high—one for the gaming system and the top one for the television—but it was better than what he'd had. "That's it. You have a TV stand."

"Sweet." He pushed it into the space they'd emptied for it.

"That was one of the first things Grandpa taught me to build. His house wasn't really well suited for raising a kid. I needed some things for my room. We built a shelf like this for my stuff to sit on."

"Mom always made him sound like a massive dick," Lonnie said as he set his television on the top shelf.

Taylor shrugged. "I guess he could be if it was warranted. I never would have crossed him. I know a few guys did and lived to regret it. I don't know that I'd say he was a massive dick, though. I'm sure Mom remembers it differently." After a few seconds, she shook her head. "It's so weird to talk about

Mom in the present tense. She was always some distant memory that I never could quite believe was real. Like...a monster under my bed or something."

Lonnie dropped to the floor to sit and added his gaming system to the shelf. "She kind of is a monster under the bed. Not the kind that wants to eat your organs, but the kind that wants to screw with your head."

"Yeah, she's good at that."

He stopped messing around with his game system components and met her gaze. "I'm sorry she said all that stuff when you found her, about not wanting to get to know you. I know she sucks, but I bet that still must have hurt."

Taylor swallowed at the stabbing in her heart. "Yeah. It was expected, though. And I'm better off without her. She was right about that."

"Doesn't make it any easier to hear."

"How do you deal with knowing she's out there and just doesn't care about us?"

He shrugged and went back to his task of stacking his games next to the console. "It pisses me off, but I can't change it. I can't change her, so I don't let it bother me. If she wants to live her life for herself, let her. She just better not come crawling when she's old, broke, and needs a place to stay. I'll send her ass to the closest shelter. She has no use for me now? Then I'll have no use for her later."

"Turnabout is fair play," Taylor acknowledged. "But I don't think she'd come to either of us. I think she'd find someone to swindle into taking her in."

He glanced at her. "She'd totally tell them we are ungrateful bastards who neglect her after all she did for us."

Taylor batted her eyes and let her shoulders sag as she

impersonated and woeful Susan O'Shea. "I gave and gave and gave, and look what they've done. Nowhere to be seen."

Lonnie joined in by softening his voice. "They never write. They never call."

Taylor chuckled. "And I sacrificed so much for them."

"Yeah," he said, returning his voice to normal. "That's totally going to happen in like twenty years."

"Totally," she agreed.

Standing up, Lonnie took a few steps back and admired his new piece of furniture. "This is awesome. Thanks, sis."

The term of endearment made her spine straighten. A slow smile curved her lips. "You're welcome."

"So I'm thinking pizza," Lonnie said. "And beer."

She was starving, and not for another frozen pizza and cheap beer, but she didn't want Lonnie to feel guilty about not being able to afford more. She wanted steaks at a steakhouse, and covering his dinner was a small sacrifice.

"Absolutely not," she stated firmly. "We're getting a meal. A real meal. Let me clean up, and then we're finding a restaurant to sit in. My treat."

Lonnie hesitated before shrugging. "Okay."

Taylor took a quick shower to wash away the walk they'd had earlier and the dust from building his shelf. She was in an unusually good mood as she walked into the bedroom where she'd been crashing. Right up until she caught her brother—*half* brother—standing over her open duffle bag. In one hand he held the envelope from her bank. In the other he held cash.

Time stopped as he looked at her with wide eyes. For a moment, she wanted to believe that he was returning the rent money she'd given him, but they'd already taken that to the property management office. She'd watched him slide that money across the desk to pay the remainder of his rent.

The money in his hand wasn't the cash she'd handed him.

The money in his hand wasn't money she'd given him.

The money in his hand was being stolen from her.

"I was putting it back," he said with a fast panicked tone. "I was putting it back." Repeating his excuse didn't make it any better, and he seemed to realize that as soon as the words left him. Lifting his hands, as if to show some kind of innocence, he continued. "I took some cash last night after you fell asleep, but I knew it was wrong, and I'm putting it back."

Taylor felt like she'd been punched in the gut. Breathing hurt. Her chest was so tight that breathing actually hurt.

He'd stolen from her. Her brother had stolen from her.

The bond she'd felt from the moment she saw him trotting down the stairs shattered like a bottle smashing to the floor. Disappointment washed over her like a rainstorm.

She wasn't disappointed in him, though. On some level, she'd expected this from him. Deep down in her gut, she'd known the truth about him. She'd been ignoring red flags right up to that point. She couldn't ignore this one. She couldn't pretend that she hadn't known what he was like before she'd ever met him.

He really hadn't had a choice.

The disappointment was in herself. For ignoring her instinct and ignoring the warnings her friends had been giving her and trusting him. She'd trusted him. She'd actually let herself believe that he wasn't going to be like the parents who'd raised him.

What a fucking foolish notion that had been.

She snatched the envelope and the cash from him without a word and counted the bills. It was there. All of it.

After stuffing it back into the bag, she grabbed the handles and yanked it off the bed as she scanned the room for her belongings.

"Don't leave," Lonnie begged, following her out of the room.

She walked into the bathroom and grabbed her shampoo bottle from the shower. She turned, and the rage she'd been trying to control unleashed. She sent the bottle flying in his direction. He put his arms up and deflected it. But then she grabbed the bottle of conditioner. That one hit him on the forehead.

"You're just like her!" With one hand, Taylor shoved him to move him out of the doorway, then stormed by him, leaving her toiletries on the floor where they landed. She could buy more shampoo.

"Taylor," he called from right behind her.

Grinding her teeth, she tightened her hold on the straps of her duffel bag so she didn't punch the lying thief right in the nose. As much as she wanted to, she reminded herself that he wasn't worth the trouble of going to jail for assault. Instead, she marched into the kitchen and dropped her bag by the fridge. Yanking it open, she started grabbing the groceries she'd bought.

"What are you doing?" Lonnie asked with a tone of disbelief.

"I bought all this," she explained as she dropped a pack of burger into her bag. "You don't get to keep it."

"Okay," he said hesitantly, "but you're putting raw meat in your bag with your clothes."

"Shut up," she snapped. The last thing she wanted was to hear his logical observation. Hell yes, she was putting raw meat into her bag. Because she'd bought that raw meat. And those clothes and that bag. She'd bought them, and he couldn't keep them.

Her bag was overflowing when she stood and almost too heavy to carry, but she managed. She had toned arms and a strong back from years of working. She wasn't a crook or a liar or a panhandler. Years of hard work, being self-reliant, and doing a damn job had made her strong. She could carry this bag.

What she couldn't do was contain the anger boiling inside her. She was in the living room when she noticed the TV stand that she'd built. With wood that she'd bought.

"Taylor," he half warned and half pleaded as she crossed the room.

She ignored him as she dropped the duffle bag and grabbed the TV and then carelessly dropped it onto the stained carpet. She grabbed the side of the stand and gave it a hard yank. The gaming system slid until it fell off the shelf along with the games.

"Don't do that," he moaned but didn't do anything to stop her.

With the shelf in one hand and the overstuffed duffle in the other, Taylor walked to the front door. Turning, she looked back at him. In that moment, seeing him looking wide-eyed and pathetic as he stared back, her anger softened. Not out of some misguided sense of forgiveness, but because in that instant, she realized that he simply had never been taught better.

Taylor deserved better than some lowlife who would take without caring of the harm he was doing.

She deserved to be treated better than he'd treated her. His lies and manipulations were his choices.

Walking away was hers.

She stopped in the doorway and looked back at him. Her anger softened as she saw the pathetic look on his face. He couldn't help how he was. He really couldn't. But she couldn't stand there and ignore that he was capable of taking something from her.

"I hope you get yourself together, Lonnie," she said sincerely. "Life is a lot better when you grow up and start taking responsibility for yourself."

With that bit of sisterly wisdom, she left him standing there. Storming down the stairs, she nearly stumbled from the awkward heavy load she was carrying. As she reached the first floor, she noticed one of Lonnie's neighbors sitting on a chair smoking by his front door. Rather than carry the TV stand and the bag of groceries to her truck, Taylor marched to the man.

"Here," she stated as she put the TV stand down.

He drew a puff off his cigarette as she opened her bag.

"This is for you," she said. "And this." She started unloading the food. "Burgers, beef tips. Chicken. You like chicken?" she asked.

"Yeah." He exhaled a cloud of smoke as he watched her.

Taylor considered for a moment that she probably looked like a lunatic, but she didn't care. As she set the last of the groceries—half a gallon of milk and a pack of hot dogs—

onto the stand, she stood up and then hefted her bag over her shoulder.

"Enjoy," she said and continued her journey toward her truck.

She climbed in, tossed her much lighter duffle bag into the passenger seat, and started her truck. As she glanced back in the mirror, she saw Lonnie coming down the stairs. Though his voice was muffled, she could hear him calling her name.

Her heart pounded in her chest and bitter tears stung the backs of her eyes. The surge of anger was already fading, and that far too familiar sense of betrayal was setting in. Once again, her trust had been abused and broken. She'd been stupid to trust him given his past, but she'd let her mind be clouded by the idea of having a family. That had been foolish. She should have known better. She had known better. She'd just ignored what she knew because she wanted so badly to be connected to someone. That was stupid.

Rather than wait to hear what he had to say, she revved the engine and squealed her tires as she backed out of the spot.

Once she pulled away, she didn't look back again.

TEN

SEVEN HOURS after leaving Lonnie's crappy apartment complex, Taylor parked outside of the house she'd been renting for the last three years. The small one-story ranch seemed more rundown than usual. Though she'd only been gone a few days, the grass was too high. The bushes needed to be trimmed. The paint, which she'd been fighting the urge to fix since it was a rental, was peeling, and one of the screens had needed to be replaced since she'd moved in.

She wouldn't call her landlord a slumlord, but he could step up his game.

So could she, if she were being honest with herself. Since she'd started making a steadier income with the new business, Darby and Jade had been urging her to move someplace nicer. They told her she'd earned it and had even pointed out some places they thought she'd like.

She'd been resistant to the idea. Up until now.

Seeing how dysfunctional her rundown rental looked, she finally came to agree with them. She deserved a nicer home. She deserved stability and respect and all those things she somehow thought she wasn't good enough to get.

She was done living in the shadow of who her mother was and what the woman had done all those years ago. Her recent visit to Susan had dashed that deep-seated hope that maybe, someday, she and her mother would have some kind of normal relationship. Lonnie's behavior had killed any hope of finding any other existing family that she could bond with. She was on her own. As she'd always been.

The long drive back from Columbus had given her plenty of time to think about what she did and didn't want out of this life—and why she'd allowed Lonnie to manipulate her into treating him like a real brother.

She had been so desperate to belong that she'd let herself get swindled even though she was smarter than that. Hadn't that been life lesson number one from her mother? *Never get attached to anyone or anything, because you'll always be disappointed.*

That wasn't a lie. Susan hadn't been wrong. Every single time in her life that Taylor had been let down was tied to someone she had counted on. Her mom. Her grandpa. Her ex-husband. And now her so-called brother.

But then Taylor thought of Jade and Darby. They hadn't let her down. In fact, they were the only two people in the world who Taylor thought she could count on no matter what. For cripes' sake, they flew out to Arizona to nurse her through confronting her mother. And she knew as soon as she could bring herself to confide how Lonnie was just as big a grifter, Jade and Darby would offer the same kind of support and comfort.

Considering how her friends always came through for

her made Taylor see that Susan *had* been wrong. It wasn't the getting attached that led to heartache, it was getting attached to the wrong people. People who lied as easily as they breathed. People who only cared about looking out for themselves.

People like her mom and brother.

Taylor was sure that by now, Lonnie had somehow convinced himself that it was Taylor's fault he'd stolen from her. He had probably found a way to blame her before he'd even sneaked into her room and sorted through her bag for the cash.

Because that's what liars and thieves and master manipulators did. They made messes and then pointed their fingers at everyone else. Susan never took responsibility for her actions, and Taylor suspected Lonnie never would either.

She had been foolish to give him a pass when she'd found out he had spent time in jail for theft. As soon as Jade and Darby had disclosed that, she should have turned her back on the idea of finding a decent member of her family.

Grimacing, Taylor slammed her head into the headrest and cursed her bad luck.

Lonnie had stolen. From her. His sister. Sure, they hadn't known each other long, but she was still his sister. She had been generous and accepting with him. And he'd stolen from her.

The asshole.

She grabbed the duffel bag from the seat beside her and headed inside. She needed a hot shower to wash away the stiffness from her long drive. Then she needed a cold beer and a burger with everything. And fries. She needed a heaping pile of fries soaked in vinegar, seasoned salt, and ketchup.

The one trip she took with her grandpa to Ocean City, they'd splurged and bought a large cup of fries. The kiosk had vinegar and seasoned salt as condiments. Neither had ever tried the combination, but once they did, Taylor was sold. That became her go-to comfort food. Harper's Ice Cream was a close second.

She needed to be comforted right now.

She was just unlocking her front door when her phone pinged.

Home yet? Darby had texted in the group chat that the three of them used. The very one where Taylor had texted to let them know she was headed back to Chammont Point and no, she didn't want to explain why. She just needed them to know to expect her to get there late.

Taylor pushed her front door open and kicked it closed behind her as she used her thumb to type back her response. *Walking in right now.*

Hungry? Darby asked almost immediately. *I can bring over burgers and fries from that place you like.*

Do you need beer? Jade asked, chiming in.

Dropping her bag carelessly at her feet, Taylor gave her head a slight shake as she smiled. She loved her friends. Despite her initial attempts at keeping them on the outside when they'd first met, they'd come to know her so well. When Jade was going through her brand of hell, they'd spent a lot of time learning how to be there for her. By the time Darby had stumbled with her wedding boutique, they knew pizza and buffalo wings would do the trick for her.

Now that Taylor had fallen flat on her face, burgers and fries were going to be the main dish.

Yeah. She loved them.

Yes to both, she responded. *Getting in the shower. Let yourselves in.*

She emptied her bag into the laundry, even though she hadn't worn all the clothes she'd packed. Everything felt dirty from being at Lonnie's place. She needed to cleanse anything he may have touched of the stench of his betrayal.

As she shook the bag over the basket, an unopened pack of cheddar cheese slices fell out. She stared at it for several seconds before picking it out of the pile of clothes. Holding it, now warm and soft from being in her bag, she frowned as she recalled cleaning out his fridge and the way Lonnie's neighbor had silently watched her empty the bag at his side.

Okay. That hadn't been her finest hour. But she'd been hurt and had responded without thinking. How should she have reacted? What should she have done?

Smiled and told him no problem. Told him no damage had been done.

That would have been a lie. A huge lie. A lot of damage had been done.

She'd told him earlier that day that she couldn't abide lies and stealing. He'd done both. So, no, storming out and taking her food and the TV stand she'd built might not have been classy, but he'd deserved it for what he'd done.

Some brother he turned out to be.

"Dickhead," she muttered as she reached into the shower to start the hot water. She stripped and stepped in as steam started rolling. The water was so hot, she hissed and automatically jolted from the shock, but she didn't alter the temperature. She suffered through the heat as if that would help wash away the cloud that had fallen over her.

Taylor couldn't recall the last time she'd felt so dim-witted. Probably not since her divorce. She'd certainly let that jackass make a fool of her. He'd blinded her with all that gross stuff that Taylor had never thought she wanted. Pretty words. Flowers. Terrible attempts at cooking her dinner.

He'd been so charming. So perfect. Too perfect. And that should have been the biggest red flag of all. She'd vowed to never fall for a man's lies ever again. But that was before she realized they were coming from her brother.

Despite the fact that Darby and Jade had seen through him, Taylor had chosen not to. Well, she wasn't ignoring the signs now. She was looking right at him and seeing him for exactly what he was.

Susan O'Shea's son.

"Idiot," she muttered into the stream of hot water, though she wasn't sure if she meant herself or Lonnie. Maybe both.

By the time she left the shower, her skin was bright red, and she felt a little lightheaded from the high temperature. After dragging a towel over her skin, she pressed her palms on the counter and took some deep breaths. The shower had definitely helped clear her head of the disappointment she felt in Lonnie. But now anger was setting in again.

Grinding her teeth, Taylor swiped the condensation from the mirror and looked at her reflection. Her eyes had taken on that hard, unforgiving look that used to be so familiar. Resting bitch face. That's what so many people had called it over the years. She had that look mastered without even trying.

However, over the last two years, she'd softened. Her

rough edges had been filed down, and the perpetual anger on her face had eased. She'd even learned to trust, thanks to her friends. There had always been a voice in the back of her mind warning her that trusting people made her vulnerable, but she'd silenced that voice. She'd ignored it. Even when it screamed at her that reconnecting with her so-called family was a huge mistake.

Thanks to Lonnie, the suspicion that had always lingered in the back of her mind came to the forefront. Worse than the suspicion that came so naturally to her, was the frustration she felt at herself. She'd been a fool to so blindly trust him. She'd let her guard down and had gotten taken advantage of. Despite a lifetime of knowing not to be so damn naïve, she had, and she'd been reminded why she didn't do that. Why she didn't make mistakes like that.

Jade and Darby were the exceptions. Those were the only two people she could count on. She certainly had tested them often enough in the past few years—and they always came through for her. They never abandoned her or gave up on helping her overcome her past.

But Lonnie... Taylor rolled her head back and exhaled slowly as she tried to remind herself that she couldn't change what had happened. She'd made a mistake trusting him. She wouldn't do that again.

"Hey," Jade called from the other side of the door. "We're here with food. Come on."

Despite the mental ass-kicking she'd been giving herself, she smiled slightly. "Be there in a sec."

"You okay, honey?" Jade asked with that overly sweet mama voice she usually saved for Darby.

Tears sprang to Taylor's eyes at the kind support she

hated so damn much. "Yeah." Her voice came out thick with emotion. Damn it. She hated feeling emotional more than she hated Jade's tendency to lay on compassion with a trowel.

Jade knocked lightly. "Tay? Can I come in?"

"I'll be out in a minute, Jade. Just...just give me a minute. Please."

When Jade didn't press, Taylor sniffled and looked into the mirror again. The fog was already starting to settle back on the space she'd cleared. That was okay. That was more than okay, actually. Because tears had filled her eyes, and the last thing she wanted was to see herself looking so weak.

She blinked several times and then rubbed the towel over her hair and squeezed out the excess water. After roughly yanking a brush through her hair, she pulled it into a soggy bun and yanked on a pair of sweatpants and a tank top. One more big, deep breath, and she pulled the bathroom door open.

"There she is," Darby said excitedly as Taylor walked into the living room.

Taylor swallowed hard so the self-pity that had been trying to overcome her since leaving Lonnie looking like a sad little puppy didn't win. As Jade and Darby had been pounding into her head for the last few years, trusting wasn't the mistake—the mistake was made by those who took advantage.

Taylor sat on the sofa between Darby and Jade. As Darby emptied the bag and checked to make sure everyone got the right order, Jade stared at Taylor. Not staring, exactly. Assessing. The worried-mom look was boring into Taylor's soul, and she couldn't help but feel the pull. That look was usually reserved for Darby, but now that it was aimed at Taylor, she felt herself crumbling.

Her lip trembled. Her eyes filled with tears. And for the first time since walking out on Lonnie, she allowed herself to accept that her heart was breaking. The pain surrounded her like a bear hug that she couldn't escape. She sniffled and swallowed hard, but hard as she tried, big tears slipped from her eyes and fell down her cheeks.

She didn't even bother wiping them away, because she knew there were more on the way.

"He stole from me," she whispered, and the air felt like it'd been sucked from the room.

Jade sighed and Darby stopped sorting food. They didn't have to be told that was the ultimate sin for Taylor. The biggest betrayal. The most unforgivable act one could commit.

"I caught him red-handed," Taylor continued. "He got into my bag, rooted around for an envelope of cash, and was standing there with money in his hand."

"I'm so sorry," Jade said.

Taylor shrugged. "You guys were right."

"We didn't want to be," Jade offered softly.

"I know," Taylor said as thickness returned to her voice. She accepted a napkin from Darby and finally wiped her cheeks. "I don't know why I thought this would end any other way. But...at least I tried, right? I tried to find my family, and it didn't work. It just didn't work, but I tried." She swiped roughly at her cheek to dry another round of tears.

Jade looked sorrowful and pressed her lips together as if she didn't want to say what she was thinking, but Darby ran her hand over Taylor's back and gave her half a hug.

"Want me to make him swim with the fishies?" Darby asked. "I know a guy. Nobody would ever suspect you."

Taylor smiled lightly but shook her head. "No. He isn't worth the trouble."

"He isn't," Jade agreed.

"I'd still do it," Darby said, sounding more sincere. "Because he deserves it."

"Yeah," Taylor agreed, "he does. But I think I'll save that favor for someone else. I stormed out. I left him standing there trying to talk his way out of it. That's all there is to it. It's done."

"He doesn't deserve you," Jade said softly.

"That's right," Darby agreed. "He isn't good enough to call you sister. That's a sacred title, and I'll wash his mouth out with soap if he ever calls you that again."

A quiet laugh left Taylor. "What'd you bring to eat?" she asked, redirecting the conversation. She leaned forward and opened her container while Darby ran down the order she'd placed. Meanwhile Jade, though she didn't drink, expertly popped the tops off two beers—one for Taylor and one for Darby—and then twisted the top of a bottle of green tea for herself.

"I want to move," Taylor announced after taking a sip from her drink.

Silence hung over them for a few beats.

"You guys are right," she continued. "I've been working hard, and I deserve to upgrade my living arrangements. I want to buy a cabin on the water."

Jade sighed. "Oh, I thought you meant you were leaving Chammont Point."

Darby blew out a breath and pressed her hand to her heart. "Me too. Sweet Jesus, boo. Don't do that to me."

"Sorry," Taylor said as she sprinkled her fries with the packet of seasoned salt Darby had picked up. "I knew what I meant."

"A cabin on the lake," Darby said. "Let me see." She immediately opened her phone and started scrolling through the houses listed for sale on the lake.

Every one that was in Taylor's budget needed some kind of work, but Taylor didn't mind. In fact, she thought she'd prefer to have something she could make her own. Though Darby was doing her best to distract from the darker issue they all knew was lingering in their minds, Jade continually looked at Taylor. Once again assessing her.

Taylor had seen her do that to Darby a hundred times. She was silently gauging her mood, her responses, and mental and emotional states. Taylor would be mad if it were anyone other than Jade.

Despite what she'd just been through with Lonnie, and the hard reminder that misplaced trust was easily abused, Taylor wasn't offended by Jade's unspoken intrusion. In fact, she appreciated it. She appreciated that someone cared enough to be concerned.

"Do you care where on the lake?" Darby asked as she scrolled her screen with one hand and ate fries with the other.

"Ideally," she confessed, "I'd like to be in the cove with you guys, but since that isn't possible, I'd settle for anywhere that allowed me to see the water. It doesn't have to be a great view, but I want to be able to sit on the porch in the evening and watch the sun set over the lake."

A wistful smile touched her lips as she considered what her grandfather would think of that. He'd say she was living beyond her means and didn't need some highfalutin cabin with a view. He'd say she was a fool to even consider putting that kind of money into a home, but Taylor brushed those thoughts aside.

She was finally going to start treating Chammont Point like this was her home instead of some place she was passing through. She was going to settle down and accept that she had a future here—instead of always running from the past.

Taylor cursed under her breath when she parked in front of the reno house early the next morning. The door was wide open. Some looters had probably kicked the door in and taken all her supplies while she was off trying to bond with her loser of a brother.

Opening the toolkit in the back of her truck, she grabbed a hammer—just in case—and marched toward the house. Her stride didn't slow until she walked inside and heard movement in the kitchen.

Clutching the hammer handle, she quietly made her way across the living room more than ready to kick the living crap out of someone. Once she made it to the kitchen, she stopped and stared. Sometime while she was in Ohio getting lied to and betrayed, someone had put white cabinets in place of the red and painted over the obnoxious yellow walls with white primer. Someone had been working on her project in her absence.

"What the hell?" she muttered. Though she'd made some

calls to a few workers she'd used before, she hadn't been able to get anyone lined up. Who the hell had been working on the house?

"Hey, Taylor."

She spun, hammer raised high, until she faced a man standing directly behind her.

Finn smirked but didn't even bother to try to lift his hands to defend himself. "I guess Jade forgot to tell you I was here," he said.

Lowering the hammer, she said, "Someone forgot to tell me something."

"Jade asked me to finish up the kitchen while you were gone. She and Darby were pretty concerned about the project falling behind."

Taylor jolted. Jade hadn't told her that. In fact, Jade had reassured her over and over that she should take all the time she needed. She'd lied? Why would Jade lie? "Jade was concerned so you just popped in to...*what*? Take over?"

"To help." Finn leaned against the counter and tilted his head. "You had some kind of family something or rather, right?"

"Yeah. Something or rather."

"Jade and Liam knew that was important to you, but they also know how important it is to move forward with the work. They didn't know how long you would be in Cincinnati."

"Columbus," she corrected.

He smirked. "*Ohio*. And every day that work isn't being done, your company is taking a loss."

Taylor cocked a brow at him. "Do not lecture me—"

"I'm not lecturing," Finn said. "I'm stating the obvious.

You were dealing with family *something or other*, and your partners were concerned about losing money. I offered to come in and help out. They accepted my offer." He gestured over his shoulder. "Now you have white walls, and your cabinets have been installed. You could say thanks."

"Thanks," she muttered.

"That almost sounded sincere."

"It almost was." Taylor reached into her back pocket and pulled out her phone as she kept an eye on him, watching him sip from a reusable coffee cup that said something about how he'd rather be surfing. She dialed Jade, and the call barely connected before Jade was rushing out an apology.

"Shit, I meant to tell you about Finn last night," she said. "I got distracted and forgot. I'm sorry, Tay. I'm so sorry. But when you said you might stay longer than a few days, we decided we had to move forward with the project."

Taylor blew out her breath. She couldn't blame them, but damn it. "Why didn't you tell me?"

"We didn't want you to feel like you had to rush home. What you were doing was important."

"So is our business."

"Yes, but family is more so," Jade insisted. "Look, I just dropped Darby off for her flight to California. I'll be back in Chammont Point in an hour or so. I'll drop by and clear the air."

Frowning at the Liam wannabe, Taylor sighed. "Don't worry about it, Jade. I get it."

"Hey," she said softly. "We weren't trying to hide what Finn was doing from you. We didn't want you to feel bad. He's good at what he does. You can trust him. And now you have some help for a few days. Real help. Put him to good use."

Taylor was glad Darby wasn't in the car for that comment. She didn't have to think too much to hear Darby twisting that around and laughing at her own jokes. After ending the call without saying goodbye, she stuffed the phone back into her pocket.

"All right, Finn," she stated flatly. "Jade says I have a few days of your assistance. I plan on using it."

He lifted his brows. "Use away."

She led him to the master bath and put him to work on tiling the floor. That was a task she had never cared for. While he did that, she started painting the bedrooms the soothing almond shade that Darby had selected. Darby didn't care for the bland color herself, but she'd compromised on her color schemes when it came to ReDo. She understood not everyone had the same taste and had accepted neutral and on-trend colors as her primary palette when it came to the remodels.

As Taylor was using the drill to stir the five-gallon bucket of paint, her phone rang. She suspected Jade had already called Darby and given her the news that they'd forgotten to update Taylor about her new assistant. Darby was probably calling first to apologize and then to tell Taylor how cute she thought Finn was.

However, when Taylor pulled her phone free, it was Lonnie's name on her screen. Her heart twisted around itself before dropping to her feet. A strange sense of anxiety rushed through her and caused her stomach to tighten. She was transported back to the moment she caught him standing over her duffel bag. Her chest felt just as tight, and she felt just as shocked.

He was calling her? Really? And he thought she would answer so she could hear more of his lies?

"Fuck you," she muttered under her breath as she ignored his call.

Almost immediately, he texted her. *I'm sorry. Please call me.*

Taylor frowned as she held down the button on the side of her phone until the option to turn off the device appeared on the screen. She tapped Shut Down, stuffed the phone back into her pocket, and focused much more than necessary on preparing to paint.

ELEVEN

THAT EVENING, with Darby in California, Finn had found his way to sitting in her usual seat around the firepit overlooking the cove. He was staying with Jade and Liam, so as long as Taylor was hanging out with them, she was hanging out with Finn.

She tried to be irritated by that, but he had turned out to be handy to have around on the job site. No one else she'd hired to help with renovations was reliable, but for the last three mornings, Finn had been at the house before Taylor. And when she got there, he was always already hard at work. She couldn't decide how she felt about that. On one hand, she really appreciated that she didn't have to hound him. But she was so used to having to treat men like unruly teenagers, she didn't know what to think about one that actually followed through.

That was weird. *He* was weird.

"Oh, my gosh," Jade said loudly as she sank into the chair next to Taylor. "I have the worst cramps right now."

"Okay," Finn said, practically jumping up and rushing

toward the water where Liam was checking something on his canoe.

Jade laughed and scooted her Adirondack chair closer to Taylor. "I thought that'd get rid of him."

"Good to know the slightest hint of female issues sends him running." Taylor stared at her friend, noting the conspiratorial look in Jade's eyes. "Why'd you get rid of him?"

"How's he working out?"

"He does what he's told."

Jade nodded. "Good. And he does it well?"

"For the most part."

"And he's reliable?" Jade asked.

Oh, shit. The light bulb in Taylor's brain flickered. "So far," she answered.

"Good," Jade said. "Because I think we need someone more…permanent…to help you. You can't handle every reno project alone, and it's been a nightmare finding help. It's too much for us to keep piling on you."

"I don't mind," Taylor stated.

"Well, I do. I don't want you to get burned out. And since Finn is reliable and does what he's told, we should hire him. Don't you think?"

The last part might have been formed as a question, but Taylor understood it really wasn't. Jade had already made up her mind. Even if Taylor disagreed, somehow or another, Finn would end up working for them.

Taylor rolled her head back. "How did I not see this coming sooner?" Turning her face toward Jade, she sighed. "Does he know this was a trial run?"

"Kind of."

"And by 'kind of,' you mean…"

Jade shrugged. "I mean he said he hoped it would turn into something permanent. He likes Chammont Point, and he likes the work."

"Does he know he'd be working with me? Every day?"

Jade grinned. "You're not as off-putting as you try to be. You know that, right?"

"Whatever," Taylor muttered. She was off-putting enough, and she was no longer ashamed by that. Being off-putting kept people away, and at the moment, Taylor wasn't really interested in having people around. People sucked.

"He's done this type of work before," Jade continued, "so he knows there would be downtime between projects. He offered to help Liam out at the store during those times. He knows what he's getting into."

"Finn wants to move to Chammont Point?" Taylor asked flatly.

"Yeah. It's been good for Liam to have him around. They've been friends since they were kids. Liam trusts him, so I trust him. And I think you can too."

Taylor shook her head. Why did she feel like she'd been set up for this? "Did you know you were going to ask me to hire him when you asked him to help?"

"No," Jade said firmly. "But when you didn't kick him off your job site, and he commented that he thought he'd like to move here, it was too perfect to pass up. Obviously, you guys can work together, and you both need that. What do you think?"

Taylor glanced at the man in question, watching him guzzle a beer on the beach as Liam cheered him on like they were in college instead of grown men. "I think it's easy to look good for the first few weeks. We should finish this project, maybe the next, and if he's still working out, we consider what we can afford to pay him for longer-term work."

"Fair enough," Jade said. After a few seconds, she added, "Finn thinks you're super focused."

Tearing her eyes from the man in question, Taylor creased her brow at Jade. "What does that mean?"

"Oh, you know, when you're working, you're completely focused on that, never even look at your phone. Don't even look at texts."

"I look at yours."

Jade hesitated. "I guess he means the ones you're ignoring."

With a slight shake of her head, Taylor scoffed and rolled her eyes. "So, he's spying on me? Is that why he's really there?"

"Of course not. He commented yesterday that he was impressed with your focus. I asked what he meant, and he said that even though your phone goes off all day long, you rarely check it. So...I figure you must be ignoring someone. Is it Lonnie?"

"Yeah," Taylor said quietly. "I don't have anything nice to say to him, so..."

"Do you want to talk about it?"

"Nope."

The silence that lingered between them let Taylor know they were going to talk about it anyway. Jade always got quiet before walking through the emotional mine fields she tended to get them all into.

"How are you feeling about all this now that you've had some time to process it?"

Taylor kept quiet for a minute. She wasn't the whiny type. Most of the time. But she felt like she'd been outright pouting about her family being such pieces of crap. She didn't want to dwell on it anymore. She couldn't change it. She couldn't fix it. All she could do was accept that they'd never live up to her expectations—which she didn't think were very high considering the biggest rule she had was to not steal.

Finally, she said, "I'm feeling like an idiot. Like I knew better but did it anyway. Like…I come from such a long line of losers that I don't even know how I'm not like them."

"Your grandfather broke that cycle for you," Jade said. "I know he was an ass at times, Taylor, but he pulled you out of that cycle. He taught you how to stand up without taking from others. I would guess that Lonnie didn't have that. Not that I'm making excuses for him," Jade was quick to add. "I just mean, you might have come from a long line of losers, but your grandfather's brand of loser was rough and tough instead of theft." She twisted her lips and scrunched up her nose. "That sounded cheesy, didn't it?"

"Oh, no. Not at all," Taylor said with a laugh before sipping her drink. As she lowered the bottle, her smile softened. "But you're right. He pushed me hard to learn what I needed to know to get me here. He wasn't easy to get along with, but he wasn't cruel. He protected me from the guys who thought a girl didn't belong on a work site. He had my back. Which is more than I can say about my mom."

"I'm sure he was trying to make up for the mistakes he'd made with your mother. Parents…decent ones anyway…don't go through life without feeling like they messed up somewhere along the way. I'm sure he thought her issues were his fault, or at least some of them."

"I'm sure," Taylor agreed softly, certain that Jade was thinking of the mistakes she felt she'd made as a mother. No matter how much her kids reassured her she hadn't messed up, Jade still felt bad that she'd spent so much of their lives focused on her career. She felt like she'd missed so much, but Taylor and Darby still didn't believe Jade's parenting was as bad as she thought. After all, Jade's kids had turned out great.

Taylor looked out at the cove. Now that Liam and Finn had wandered off to do something else, she could watch the water softly lap ashore and birds ride the breeze without being distracted by their constant goofing off. The scene should be peaceful. She usually loved sitting here like this, watching the world go by. But on this particular evening, there was a storm brewing in her mind. She'd been trying to ignore it for days, but every time Lonnie reached out, she felt thunderclaps shake her to the core.

At first, it was the anger that shook her, but that had slowly started to turn to something she couldn't quite name. Now that she'd had a few days to calm down, she was starting to see a different side of the situation.

"Lonnie didn't have someone to help him break the cycle, as you called it," Taylor said. "He grew up with two completely dysfunctional parents. He said he'd leave for a while when things got bad, but I didn't ask what he meant by 'bad.' I don't know what all he grew up witnessing, but I'm pretty sure that he's doing what he knows. Lying, cheating, and stealing are staples of our mother's personality."

"That's true."

Taylor frowned as heaviness settled in her chest. "I'm his sister."

"Also true," Jade said softly.

Looking at Jade, Taylor voiced the question that had been nagging her. "So, I've been starting to think that... Maybe..." She pressed her lips together for a few seconds before asking Jade, "Is it my responsibility to help Lonnie like Grandpa helped me?"

Jade took a deep breath but didn't answer. She was considering her words. She did that whenever she was going to say something she thought someone wouldn't like. Deep breath, glazed-over eyes, and then *pow*! Truth bomb.

"Come on," Taylor moaned after several drawn-out seconds. "You're the mother hen here. You're supposed to know these things. Am I responsible for getting Lonnie on track?"

"No," Jade stated. "He's an adult. He's responsible for himself. If he hasn't learned his lesson after a stint in jail, I'm not sure what you can do for him."

Taylor waited because she sensed there was a *but* coming.

"But," Jade said, "you have a valid point. He didn't have someone like your grandpa to straighten him out. Sometimes people need to understand someone is there for them, to show them there's a different way, before they can get on the right path. If Lonnie's never had that, I don't see how anyone can expect him to find his way."

Taylor dropped her head back. "Damn it. I have such a shitty track record with people like that. You know? Shutting him out seemed like the right thing at first, but now I don't know. Do I give him another chance? If I did, will he take it or will he lie again? How do I know? How am I supposed to trust him when I know he betrayed me? What am I supposed to do?"

"Those are all really good questions. Unfortunately, I can't answer any of them," Jade said. "I can't tell you what you need to do. You have to decide that. You and Lonnie haven't had some lifelong connection. The only thing that binds you is a little bit of your mother's DNA. He hurt you. I know you well enough to know that forgiveness doesn't come easy. That's because you've been taught some really hard life lessons."

"Because of shit like what he did." Again, silence hung in the air as Taylor debated what, if anything, she could do to help Lonnie realize he didn't have to be like his parents. "He didn't have to choose that life," she said after several minutes.

"No, he didn't."

"I don't know that I can ever forgive him for what he did. It isn't about the money," Taylor added quickly.

"I know," Jade said with soothing reassurance. "He betrayed your trust."

"Exactly. And no matter what he says, I don't think I can get over that."

"What does he say? In his texts and voicemails?"

Taylor heaved a sigh. "I don't know. I haven't given in to the urge to check them."

"Maybe you should. Not because you'll forgive and forget but because you need answers so you can stop obsessing about it."

Taylor started to tell Jade she hadn't been obsessing but doing so was futile. Jade knew her too well. That's exactly what Taylor had been doing for days.

After downing what was left in her bottle, Taylor swiped

the screen of her phone and tapped in her password. She gave Jade one last glance before pushing herself up and walking away. She needed some space to read his texts and listen to his voicemails. She sat on the bottom stair leading up to Darby's deck so she was out of the way. The tall trees shaded her from the evening sun, making it easier to see her screen.

She scrolled through the text messages first. As she expected, most were pleas for her to call him, to answer his calls, and to hear him out.

His voicemails were much the same. He explained that he was freaked out about his finances, and he was sorry that he'd taken from her, but he had realized his mistake and really was putting the money back, which was when she'd walked in on him.

After listening to the sixth, and final, voicemail, Taylor rolled her head back to look at the sky as if she might somehow find the answers there. There was nothing there. Not even a cloud dotted the sky that was starting to turn shades of pink and purple as evening moved in.

"Hey," Finn said as he walked toward her in long strides. "Jade and Liam are headed out on the lake. I was thinking about running to the store to grab some steaks. Want one?"

"No," she said. "I'm gonna head out."

He tilted his head in the same way Jade did when she was feeling sorry for Taylor.

Taylor sighed and rolled her eyes. "What'd she tell you?"

"Nothing."

"Bullshit," Taylor stated.

Finn put his foot on the bottom step and rested his forearm on the banister as he looked around. Looked at anything but Taylor. "She said it's your brother who has been blowing up your phone and that you're trying to figure out if you can forgive him for something. She didn't say for what."

"He stole money from me," Taylor stated without thinking. She immediately regretted it. None of this was Finn's business. "We just met. I didn't know about him until a few weeks ago. And the first time we met, he stole my cash, so..." She shrugged because there wasn't much else she could say.

Finally, Finn looked down at her. "I'm sorry."

"Yeah, well, it happens." She stood and shoved her phone into her back pocket as she slid past him.

"I'm a good listener," Finn offered.

Taylor considered her words before looking up at him. "Looks like you're about to become a long-term member of my crew, Finn. I don't dump my personal shit on my crew."

He grinned. "That's not true. You've been in a piss-poor mood since I met you. I'd guess that is strictly due to your personal problems."

"Wrong," she informed him. "I've been in a piss-poor mood since the day I was born."

She left him standing there, ignoring the way he laughed at her confession. She didn't smile until she'd driven away.

Taylor had never been one for change. She didn't like the unexpected, but ever since she'd settled into life at Chammont Point, change had been inevitable. Jade and Darby had come into her life and forced her out of her comfort zone. They'd shown her what real, genuine human connection could be.

Even Liam had managed to grow on Taylor. At first, she was

worried he was only drawn to Jade because she'd been in crisis when she'd come to Chammont Point, and Liam was definitely one of those hero types. But he'd proven himself by stepping back and not pressuring Jade until she was ready to move forward. He'd earned Taylor's respect by respecting her friend. She wasn't nearly as offended by his presence as she used to be. She hadn't made up her mind about Finn yet, but she figured she still had time. From the sounds of it, he wouldn't be going anywhere, which gave Taylor an odd sense of comfort.

One of the biggest challenges she'd faced since starting her own business, even before she'd partnered to make ReDo, had been finding good help. If having Finn on board would ease some of her burden, she was ready to admit she needed that. What she didn't need was another friend checking in on her, though. Two best friends making her examine her emotions were enough.

Ten minutes later, Taylor slowed her truck down as she approached her rental. There, parked on the street outside her house, was a dented, rusted sedan with Ohio license plates. The bug-covered windshield was evidence of the long drive the car had endured.

"You have got to be fucking kidding me," she muttered as she turned into her driveway.

As she parked, a dark-haired, willowy man stood from where he'd been perched on her front stairs. Lonnie shoved his hands in his pockets and watched as she sat in her truck debating what to do. Finally, she climbed out and slammed the door behind her. Damn. He had some nerve just showing up at her house like this.

"How did you know where I live?" she asked.

He gave her a lopsided, shy grin. "I know how to use a search engine. Your address is listed in the local directory."

"Right," she said and then exhaled loudly. "What do you want?"

His smile fell, and sadness filled his eyes. "I'm sorry."

"Okay," she said flatly.

"I was trying to put the money back because I knew I screwed up."

She didn't respond. She didn't know what she was supposed to say. Even if he had put the money back, even if he had realized his mistake, he'd stolen from her.

"How do I make it better?" Lonnie asked.

His question jolted her. She hadn't been expecting that. She wasn't used to people owning up to their mistakes, let alone trying to fix them. Her mother hadn't done that. Neither had her ex.

"You broke my trust," Taylor said quietly. "You can't make that better."

"I want to try," Lonnie said. "I made a bad choice, but I realized I messed up, and I was putting the money back."

"You were putting the money back so I wouldn't catch you, Lonnie," she pointed out. "If you had actually been sorry, you would have confessed and admitted you made a mistake to my face."

He was silent for a long time. "I should have done that. You're right. I can't change what I did, but I want to try to start over."

"I'm not really good at giving second chances," Taylor admitted.

Lonnie was quiet for a long time, as if he were expecting more, but she didn't know what else to say.

"Okay," he finally said quietly. "I guess... I guess I should go, then."

"Yeah," Taylor said. "You should."

"Here." He pulled a folded piece of paper from his back pocket. "I took this the last time I moved out of Mom's place. I thought you might want this."

Taylor hesitated before taking the paper. Flipping it open, her breath caught at the image of a much younger version of her grandpa holding a little girl on his knee. Taylor didn't have any photos from her toddler years, but she recognized herself in the child. Her heart lurched to her throat, and her eyes stung as tears tried to form.

"Mom had this?" Taylor asked.

"She showed it to me once when I told her I didn't believe you were real. She had some other pictures, but this was the one I took." He smiled shyly. "I guess I just confessed to stealing again, didn't I? Maybe I am more like her than I realized. Anyway, you should have that."

Taylor opened her mouth when Lonnie walked around her, but she couldn't find the words to stop him. A minute later, she heard a car door slam and an engine start. She didn't stop him from leaving. She couldn't stop staring at the photo he'd given to her.

She couldn't have been more than one or two as she gave a big, gummy grin. There was an odd show of pride in her grandpa's eyes as he looked at her. As always, there was a cigarette and a beer in hand, but the one he had wrapped around her, holding her against his chest, gave an air of protectiveness. There was a bond between them, even in that photo. A bond that was quiet, but somehow seemed stronger than any other connection she'd ever had.

Her heart ached and her lip trembled as she finally lowered the photo. She looked down the street, but Lonnie was long gone.

Taylor walked through her house and straight to her back porch. She didn't invoke her grandfather's cigarette and coffee scent this time. She didn't think she'd want to know what he'd say. She'd heard plenty of his negative thoughts on second chances over the years.

When she'd been young and dumb enough to think her mom might return, she'd asked him what they would do on that day—the day her mom came back. Her grandfather's mood had grown dark, and he'd sat quietly for some time before speaking in a low, gravelly voice.

"Someone once said that when people show you what they are like, you'd better believe them. That's true, Taylor. If you don't ever believe anything else this old fool tells you, believe that. Your mom showed you who she is. Believe it. Second chances are earned. Not given. She hasn't done a damn thing to earn one, has she?"

Taylor hadn't been old enough to understand or answer, but she was smart enough to know that her grandpa had already answered the question. She had shaken her head, though she didn't fully grasp what he'd meant.

"Sometimes you just gotta let someone go their own way, kid," he said, satisfied with her response.

He would have said those same words about Lonnie.

Taylor didn't doubt that. She suspected he would have been right. He usually was.

Let him go, kid. That's what Grandpa would tell her. But something inside her wasn't ready to give up on her brother. There had been something redeemable in her, and she knew there was something in Lonnie. She just had to prove that to him. She had to help him see that he could be better. If it hadn't been for Grandpa teaching her that, she never would have known. She would have always been the kid of a con artist. Grandpa had taught her to be more.

Taylor looked at the phone in her hand for a long time before swiping the screen to unlock it. Then she stared even longer after finding Lonnie's contact information. After swallowing hard and taking a long breath, she tapped to call him.

His line only rang once before he answered. "Hey."

"Hey," she said.

"What's up?" he asked when she didn't say more.

"You're my brother," she said quietly, "and it would be shitty of me to give up on you that easily. So…I'll give you another chance. But if you steal so much as a penny from me again, I will write you off just like I have our mother. Do you understand that?"

"Yes," he said. That was it.

No excuses, no pleading, just confirmation that he understood. Good.

"I need help," Lonnie said. "Like…I need someone to help me, Taylor. Someone who can keep me in line until I figure things out."

She didn't argue that point. She'd talked to Jade about this no more than half an hour prior. Lonnie might *technically* be an adult, but he'd never had the kind of guidance needed to teach him responsibility. He needed someone to put expectations on him, to give him pats on the back when he was right and redirection when he was wrong.

He needed someone to invest in him, to believe in him. And who better to do that than his big sister?

Ignoring the screaming in the back of her mind, the one that sounded an awful lot like her grandfather, Taylor said, "I could use some help on this project. It's not a full-time gig, but...it'll be a steady paycheck for a few weeks. If that goes well, we can talk about the next project."

"I, uh, I could barely figure out how to use a level, Taylor. Are you sure you want me on your job site?"

She smirked. "We all have to start somewhere. You'll be doing grunt work, but it's work, Lonnie. Do you want it?"

"Yeah," he said. "I want it."

She was quiet for a few seconds. "Where are you sleeping?"

"I don't know."

"I have a couch," she offered. "It's lumpy and smells like stale beer, but you're welcome to it."

"Okay," he said. "I can be there in a few minutes."

"Lonnie," she said before he could hang up. "Don't make me regret this."

"I won't," he said.

Taylor ended the call and blew out her breath.

Somehow, she had expected to feel better about giving him a second chance.

TWELVE

THE NEXT MORNING, Taylor grabbed breakfast for Jade and herself and headed to the cove under the pretense that they needed to debate one of the properties they'd viewed and were considering purchasing. In reality, she had a few things she needed to hash out with Jade. The Greek yogurt parfait she'd picked up from the coffee shop was simply to soften the blow of what she had to say.

Taylor texted Jade when she'd arrived and had barely pulled their breakfast from the bag when Jade came bouncing out of her cabin with Darby-esque enthusiasm. She stopped about halfway to the table and looked around.

Slowing her gait, she let a frown turn her lips down. "What about Finn?"

Taylor furrowed her brow. "What about Finn?"

"I thought you'd get something for him too."

"Why would I get him breakfast? He's not part of our morning meetings."

Jade shrugged. "Well...it would be nice if you...included him more."

Taylor creased her brow as Jade oh-so-innocently sat at the table. "Included him in *what*?"

Jade shrugged and pried the top off her yogurt. "I just... I think he was pretty disappointed that you didn't want to have dinner with him last night. You know. After Liam and I decided to go out on the water. Without him."

Taylor creased her brow. "He wanted to grill steaks, Jade. He didn't ask me..." It took a few seconds for the dots to connect in Taylor's mind, but once they did, she jerked her sunglasses off her face and stared at Jade with wide eyes. "You are *not*!"

"What?" Jade asked, once again acting far too innocent. She put her hand to her chest in the way Darby did when she was completely guilty. She even widened her eyes and then blinked long and slow as if she had no idea what was happening.

Oh, yeah. Guilty.

Taylor ground her teeth together as she glared. "Are you trying to hook me up with that cheap knockoff of your boyfriend?"

Jade's mouth opened, but she was grinning behind her shock. "Cheap knockoff? What do you mean?"

"Oh, please," Taylor said and rolled her eyes. "That messy surfer wanna-be hair, the constant five o'clock shadow, and that devil-may-care attitude. He is definitely a cheap version of Liam."

"I think Finn's pretty cute." Jade's eyes were practically dancing with the amusement she was obviously finding in the situation. She'd never tried to set Taylor up before but seemed to be enjoying herself now.

Taylor wasn't sure how sincere Jade was in this endeavor,

but she wanted to put an end to it. Now. "Then take him," Taylor said with a dismissive wave of her hand. "Start one of those reverse harems that Darby's always rattling on about in those books she reads."

Jade scrunched her nose. "Ew. I already have to pick up after one messy male. I'm not willingly taking on another."

"Well, neither am I," Taylor insisted. "I think I have enough on my plate. Don't you? Besides, you added him to my crew. I'm not dating a member of my crew. That's asking for trouble."

"Yeah, I guess. But I was hoping you'd at least find him attractive."

"I don't," Taylor stated and opened the container holding her ham and cheese omelet and hash browns.

Pinching her fingers together, Jade eyed Taylor. "Not even a little?"

"No. He's cocky and...full of himself...and conceited."

"That's three different ways to say the same thing," Jade pointed out.

Taylor knew that, but she couldn't think straight. The idea that Jade had been trying to set her up had her out of sorts. Add that to the fact that she hadn't slept well the night before, and she was not prepared to dance around this conversation.

Taylor couldn't remember the last time she'd even considered dating. Men were trouble. She certainly didn't need any more of that. "I didn't come here to talk about Finn."

Tilting her head down to see over her sunglasses, Jade eyed Taylor. "I assumed you came for our morning meeting like always."

"I did, but..." She ripped open the plastic package holding the disposable eating utensils and pulled out the flimsily made fork. "You know how we were talking last night about how maybe Lonnie needs someone to help him?"

Sinking back, as if no longer interested in her breakfast, Jade nodded.

"Well, after reading his texts and listening to his apologies, I thought about it, and..."

"You called him?"

"Actually," Taylor stated as she poked at her side of hash browns, "he was sitting on my porch when I got home last night. We had a pretty good exchange of words before I sent him on his way. But then I broke down and called him back. He seemed very sincere in his apology, so I accepted and... offered to give him a second chance."

A frown toyed at Jade's lips. "You're going back to Columbus with him?"

"No." She drew a breath, bracing to tell Jade what she'd done. "I invited Lonnie to stay with me. For a while."

Jade's brows shot up, and her lips pressed into a flat line, but she didn't speak. Taylor expected her to be shocked by the news, but she wasn't even sure if Jade was breathing. The air between them grew tense, and the only sound was the soft, repetitive sloshing of waves hitting the beach. Even the birds had grown quiet.

Unable to take another second of the heavy silence, Taylor said, "He said he stole from me because he's had such a hard time finding a job and freaked out about missing some bills."

"He was having a hard time finding a job because he went to jail for theft," Jade pointed out rather bluntly.

Taylor let that observation slide. "He came all this way so he could apologize, which is more than anyone else has ever done. Mom certainly wasn't sorry, and that worthless ex of mine—"

"*Taylor*," Jade nearly screamed as she sat forward. "What is he going to do for work so he doesn't have to steal from you again?"

This was the part that Taylor had really come to discuss. Jade wasn't going to like this, but Taylor had made an executive decision, and as a partner of ReDo Realty, she was allowed to do that. Or so she'd told herself over and over the night before.

"He's going to work for us." She pointed her fork at Jade. "Before you go off on some kind of rant about hiring someone without discussing it with you first, I found out about Finn when I walked in on him working on our reno."

"Finn doesn't have a record."

"Well...he might. I mean, how well do you actually know him?"

"He *doesn't*," Jade practically spat. "He and Liam have been friends for years. Do you honestly think I'd try to set you up with someone who had a record?"

Taylor gasped. "So you admit to trying to set me up with Finn!"

"That is not the point." If Jade's clipped tone hadn't expressed her anger, the red rising up her neck and settling over her face was a serious warning. She was about to blow her top, but Taylor had prepared for that. "If you want Finn to work for us, well, I want Lonnie to work for us. We're even." As soon as Lonnie had agreed to come to Chammont

Point, Taylor had been preparing to break the news to Jade. "I'll take responsibility for him," Taylor said.

"Yes, you will," Jade stated. "And he will not have access to any accounts at ReDo. You'd better lock up that company credit card, because if he so much as charges a stick of gum without our permission—"

"He won't," Taylor said, cutting her off.

Jade had every right to be concerned, but Taylor wasn't going to listen to a lecture. Lonnie was her brother. He'd made a mistake. But Taylor said she'd vouch for him, and that should be enough for Jade. Jade didn't have to trust Lonnie, but she should trust Taylor.

"He knows he'd better not blow this," Taylor said. "He knows this is his last chance with me and *could* be his last chance at gainful employment. He's going to walk the line. Besides, I'm going to keep an eye on him."

Jade slouched her shoulders and let out a loud sigh. Her body language made it clear that she was angry and probably a little disappointed, but Taylor refused to back down. After all, it was Jade who had been telling Taylor for the last two years that she was too hard on people sometimes. Jade was the one who was all about forgiveness and moving forward. She was the one always harping on Taylor to let go of the past.

"We all deserve a second chance," Taylor said. "Even people who have been in jail." She waited for Jade to realize that Taylor had turned her words around on her.

As soon as Jade did, she gave her head a slight shake. "When I talked to you about giving him a second chance, I did not mean bring him here to play an integral role in our company. I meant try to have a sisterly relationship with him.

Call him once a week. Visit him on holidays. Send birthday cards. I did *not* mean bring him here. You caught him with your money in his hands, Taylor."

"He's not going to be around money on a renovation site."

"He didn't go to jail for stealing money. He went to jail for pawning his ex's belongings."

"I know," Taylor said softly. "But he's my brother, Jade. I have to give him a level playing field so he can try to be better. I know what his life was like. I lived it, but I got out. He didn't."

"It doesn't seem like he tried very hard."

Taylor let that comment linger before making a point she didn't like making. "You never had to try for anything. You had two parents who supported you. The biggest struggle you had was getting pregnant too young. But even then, your parents were there to catch you. You don't know what it's like to not have someone there."

Taylor knew her comment stung by the way Jade tensed and blinked but didn't argue. Taylor didn't like poking her friend like that, but she'd spoken the truth. Jade had sometimes struggled with finances when she was younger, but she'd never faced abuse and neglect, and she sure as hell didn't know what it was like to not have a safety net.

"He needs someone to give him a chance," Taylor said. "He needs someone to believe in him the way you guys believe in me even though I'm a hot mess most of the time."

Jade blew out her breath. "You're a trustworthy and honest hot mess. He's a proven liar and thief."

Taylor nodded. "I know. But I need to help him, and I need you to support me in that. Please. I have to show him life can be better than what he knows. I have to give him a chance, a real chance, to build a better life for himself. He's never had that, Jade. He's never had someone rooting for him."

Jade's face softened. "He's going to hurt you again."

"I don't think so. He was very repentant."

"Repentance doesn't mean a damn thing if a lesson hasn't been learned."

Taylor leaned back in her chair and recalled the way Lonnie sounded so shocked the night before when she'd called him and asked him to come back, like he was scared she wouldn't forgive him.

"He learned," she said.

"I hope so. I hope it wasn't just lip service to win you over."

"He's starting today," Taylor said, causing Jade to scoff softly. "I know it won't be easy, but can you guys try to be nice? No matter what you think of him, he's my brother, and he matters to me."

The muscles in Jade's jaw worked for several seconds before she heaved a sigh. "My God, the things I do for my friends," she muttered but then offered Taylor one of her maternal smiles. "Yes. I'll be nice. But if that little...jerk hurts you again, he'll wish he was back in jail."

Taylor smiled. "Thanks, Jade."

"No matter what, we're keeping Finn," Jade announced. "I like him. I *trust* him."

Scowling, Taylor opted to ignore Jade's dig at Lonnie. "Have you looked at the budget? Can we afford two helpers?"

"We'll make it work," Jade said as she yanked her fork package open. She cast a glance at Taylor. "You have to be honest with us. If Lonnie isn't working out, you have to let him go. We can't pay someone just because you want to."

Taylor held her breath, reminding herself to think before speaking. "What if it's Finn who isn't working out?"

"Finn's going to work out."

"He might not," Taylor said. "Are you prepared to fire Liam's friend?"

Sitting taller, Jade poked at her yogurt. "Yes. If he isn't working out, I'm prepared to fire him."

"And I'll fire Lonnie if he isn't working out. Okay?"

"Okay," Jade said.

Taylor took a big bite of her omelet. As she chewed, she watched Jade. Though nothing else was said about the situation, Taylor knew Jade was pissed, which made her more determined than ever to make sure Lonnie didn't screw this up. Not only did she need to prove to Jade that she'd made the right decision, but she needed her brother to prove that he was worth giving another chance.

Lonnie arrived at the renovation site right on time, and Taylor immediately put him to work cleaning up the mess from the demolition she'd been doing in the living room. She wasn't going to baby him. She wasn't going to take it easy on him. Her grandfather had always said coddling someone only enabled them. The last thing Lonnie needed was to be enabled.

However, she wasn't going to beat him down for what he'd done in the past either. She was giving him a second chance, and she was determined to make this a clean slate.

She glanced up in time for Finn to walk into the room. He watched Lonnie for a few seconds before shaking his head ever so slightly as he grabbed a box of nails off a makeshift worktable. Taylor didn't like the way Finn continually eyed her brother with an air of suspicion he had no right to have.

Taylor regretted telling Finn about Lonnie's actions. She should have kept that to herself. She wasn't usually so open, but she'd told him her problems and couldn't take back what she'd said. The lack of trust in Finn's eyes was unmistakable and made Taylor bristle. It wasn't Finn's place to watch the crew. Both of those were Taylor's responsibilities. This was her crew. She was the one who should be sharing information and determining who was and wasn't trustworthy.

Having Finn edge into that role after less than a week of working for ReDo pissed her off. She didn't care if he'd been friends with Liam for years. He'd been a member of her team for a few days. He had no right to act like it was his place to protect the job.

"Get back to work on the bathroom," she ordered him when he made yet another unnecessary trip into the living room to spy on Lonnie.

The only acknowledgment Finn gave that he'd heard her was a slight quirk to his left eyebrow before leaving them alone.

"You have to get all the debris up," Taylor continued to Lonnie. "If we put glue down on a bunch of drywall dust or nails, it's going to come loose. We don't want to get a reputation for doing shoddy work. Get it?"

"Got it?" Lonnie said as he eyed the heavy-duty shop

vacuum she'd pushed toward him. "I thought you were kidding when you said I'd be doing grunt work."

Taylor's spine straightened, and she let the words her grandfather used to say slip before she could stop them. "Grunt work still gets an honest paycheck. If you don't want it, I can give it to someone else."

"No, ma'am," Lonnie said immediately and turned on the vacuum.

She ignored the sarcastic lilt to his voice as she marched across the house. She found Finn prying open the top of a canister of grout. She skimmed the shower, impressed by how quickly he'd added the tiles, but she wasn't in the mood to compliment him or his work.

She put her hands on her hips and held his gaze. "Do we have a problem?"

Finn didn't look at her. He kept his eyes on the container as he said, "No."

His lack of eye contact seemed to imply that he was lying, but she didn't care. She hadn't actually wanted to hash out his issues. She simply wanted to make a point of letting him know that he was out of line.

"Good," she said. "Because I'm the foreman here, and I say who works on this job and who doesn't."

Again, his only acknowledgment was a slight grin as she turned to leave.

"I think it's admirable that you're trying to help your brother," Finn said.

She stopped and heaved a sigh. Spinning on her heels, she faced him. "But?"

Finally, Finn looked at her. His smile was gone now, and

sympathy had filled his eyes. "But he's going to let you down, Taylor. I hope you're prepared for that."

"This is none of your business," she said before leaving him to get to work on her own to-do list.

As she painted the ceiling of the master bedroom, she did her best to focus on the music coming from the speaker she'd synced with her phone instead of replaying Finn's warning. She suspected he was right. Lonnie was going to disappoint her. Again.

Two hours later, the painting and grout work in the bedroom and bathroom were done. Taylor told Finn to call it a day then went in to check on Lonnie. He was slow, but he'd done the job she'd asked him to do. Though she'd had to come in repeatedly to remind him to put his phone down and focus on the chore she'd given him, the living room was spotless, with two trash bags of debris sitting next to the front door.

"Let's wrap it up for today," she said when he turned off the shop vacuum.

"Thank you," Lonnie said with a miserable moan. He stretched his back then leaned from side to side as Taylor looked over the floor he'd meticulously cleaned.

"This is good," she said, opting not to mention that it should have taken him a quarter of the time it had. She'd given him a task, and he'd done it and done it well. She'd work on his speed another day. "Hungry?"

"Famished," he said.

Within an hour, they were sitting at La Cocina in a booth toward the back of the restaurant. Taylor didn't bother looking at the menu, as she knew what she intended to order.

Instead, she scarfed down tortilla chips and salsa and got her thoughts together.

Finally, Lonnie set his menu aside and smiled. "They have a jumbo margarita."

She nodded. "It's enough for two, really." Brushing her hands on her thighs, she gave herself a few more seconds before sitting back and frowning at him. "I need you to take this seriously."

"Dinner?" he asked.

"Working for me. I didn't hire you so you could slack off."

His smile fell. "I worked my ass off—"

"I'm not talking about the work you did. I'm talking about your attitude. Doing grunt work isn't beneath you, Lonnie. It isn't beneath anyone."

A scoff left him as he sat back.

"Listen to me," Taylor said. "I'm here to help you. You said you needed a job to earn money and a work history to get the job you want. I'm giving that to you. But you'll respect what I'm offering, or I'll take it away."

Damn it. She sounded just like her grandfather. He'd given her this lecture once too. Actually, he'd given it to her several times. And every time, she'd had the same *fuck you* look on her face that Lonnie was giving her now. She didn't want to have that same love-hate relationship with Lonnie that she'd had with Grandpa, but she wouldn't get walked over either.

Taking her lecture down a notch, she let her shoulders sag so she didn't come off as so aggressive. "If you work hard, in six months you can have enough money to enroll in the certification course at the community college. You can stay with me to save on rent."

The muscles in his jaw flexed as he looked away. Looking at anything but her. Yeah, she knew that look. She used to get it with her grandfather. Lonnie was doing everything he could to not tell her where to go in that moment.

"I'll help you get on your feet," Taylor said. "I'll help you. But you have to be willing to help yourself, Lonnie. You want a new life. You want to put the past behind you. This is your chance. Don't blow it."

"Where the hell is this coming from?" Lonnie asked with an angry clip to his voice.

"I just don't want you to screw this up."

"I'm not going to," he barked as he stared at her with hard eyes. Like he had the right to be offended that she would doubt him.

But she did doubt him. In between having to remind him to put his phone away, she'd had to remind him to get off his ass because nobody needed that many breaks. Then she'd had to tell him to toss out the beer he'd brought in from his trunk. When he'd protested, she'd had to remind him he was at work. And there would be no alcohol on her site.

Taylor understood that Lonnie thought he'd hit rock bottom when he'd gone to jail, but if he had, he wouldn't have tried to steal from her, and he wouldn't be acting like he was put out by the work she'd offered him. He still had so much further to fall before he woke up and understood how much growing he had to do.

Jade was right. Lonnie hadn't learned a lesson from his stint in jail.

And Finn was right. Lonnie was going to let Taylor down.

She just hoped that it wasn't the same kind of letdown that happened last time. She hoped it was more along the lines of slacker or complainer. She'd even settle for him disappearing without notice. Because if Lonnie went down the road of theft one more time, their relationship was done.

For good.

She forced a smile when their waitress stopped at their table. Despite the nagging feeling that she was going to regret extending a helping hand to Lonnie, she was determined to at least enjoy her dinner.

By the time their food arrived, the tension had faded, and Lonnie had her laughing at his description of cleaning out the vacuum bag and accidentally pouring drywall dust down his jeans. He was so animated, and his dramatic timing was spot on. It was then that she realized why she was so determined to save him. Because this was what family should be. They could have their differences, but those moments didn't have to stick around. They could have intense conversations one moment and laugh the next.

Because that's what family did. And even on his worst days, Lonnie was her family.

THIRTEEN

THREE DAYS LATER, Taylor sat in the cove admiring the green leaves slowly starting to change into red and gold as she had lunch with Darby and Jade. The overnight temperatures were beginning to dip lower and lower, but the sun still warmed the days enough to enjoy summer activities. Not that Taylor had been doing much of those this summer. Her self-inflicted family drama had robbed her of the time and energy to do many of the things she enjoyed during the warmer months at Chammont Point. She had barely found time to enjoy the water.

"I had to do it," Darby stated, wrapping up her dramatic retelling of how she'd left Noah's bed in the middle of the night and came home two days early. "I had to sneak out while he was sleeping because I couldn't possibly leave if he kept giving me those sad puppy eyes."

Darby's story pulled a giggle from Taylor, despite the dark mood that was far too common these days. Darby had only been gone a week, but Taylor had missed not hearing her friend's over-the-top reactions to everything.

"But really," Darby said, dropping her hand from her chest. "I don't think I can go back. Being together again was great, but it's only prolonging what we know will happen. At some point, one of us will get tired of waiting and end things permanently. It's better to walk away now."

"Long-distance relationships aren't for the weak of heart," Jade said.

"Relationships in general aren't for the weak of heart," Taylor offered.

Darby smiled softly before asking, "How are things going with your brother?"

Taylor considered confiding how every morning for the last three days had been a fight to get him off the couch and dressed for work. And how she was constantly reminding him to work harder and faster. She would love to complain and vent her frustrations, but she wasn't willing to let Jade know how frustrated she was. Jade might not come right out and say that she'd warned about exactly this, but Taylor didn't even want her thinking it. She hadn't gone into this expecting converting Lonnie into a hard worker would be easy.

"He still has some learning to do," she said instead, "but he's starting to figure things out."

That was a vague and yet at least somewhat accurate response. Lonnie was easy going. But sometimes he was too easy going. Bordering on lazy.

She glanced at Jade, catching the frown on her face. No doubt Finn was going home every night and filling Jade's ears full of his theory about how Lonnie was taking advantage of Taylor's kindness. Yes, she'd bought his lunch almost every day, but he hadn't been paid yet. And, yes, she'd given him a job based on his relationship to her and not on his skillset, but lots of people did that.

Maybe Lonnie was taking advantage to a point, but Taylor was confident that she was making progress on teaching him the benefits of hard work. He'd been there less than a week. They couldn't expect him to be fully pulling his weight in less than a week. He'd never done that type of work before. Once he got more comfortable with the tasks, he'd be more productive, or so she was telling herself.

Jade was still regarding her with a frown. Time to change the subject. "So, Jade," Taylor said, "when are you proposing to Liam?"

Jade immediately jerked her head around as she hushed Taylor. Once she was convinced Liam hadn't overheard, she sighed with relief. "Keep your voice down. I don't want to ruin the surprise."

"I still can't believe you're breaking tradition," Darby said.

"Says the girl who flew to California for sex," Jade countered.

Taylor gave herself a mental high-five. She'd much rather listen to Darby and Jade debate marriage proposal etiquette than have to defend her choice to hire Lonnie. Mostly because deep down inside, she feared he was going to make her regret giving him a second chance. She was trying to let go of her concerns, the ones that refused to die. He'd stolen. He'd steal again.

It's just a matter of time, the voice in the back of her mind kept whispering. That voice sounded far too much like her grandfather at times.

"That was a nice try, by the way," Jade stated as she stared at Taylor, "but you're not changing the subject that easily. We're worried about you."

"Who is we?"

"Both of us," Darby and Jade said at once.

Taylor frowned at them but resisted the urge to roll her eyes like Darby would. "I need you guys to trust me," Taylor stated with more edge than intended.

Jade widened her eyes slightly as if shocked. "We do."

"Apparently not, because you brought Finn in without consulting me, even though construction is my area. And you've done nothing but question my decision to hire Lonnie. Even though I'm the one who is supervising him. So, no. I don't think you trust me at all."

"That's not what we're saying," Jade insisted.

"That's exactly what you're saying."

Again, the cove was quiet.

"I'm sorry." Jade sounded sincere in her apology. "I never meant to imply that I don't trust you. I'm worried about you. That's all. I'm worried."

"Well, don't be," Taylor said firmly. "If Lonnie screws up, I'll handle it like I would with any other member of my crew. He's not getting special treatment. I'm not coddling him. I'm offering him a chance to do better. If he blows it, then he blows it, but it's my choice to give him the chance."

"Okay," Jade said.

Taylor scoffed as she shook her head. "You don't get it, Jade. You don't know what it's like to go through your entire life with everyone watching you, expecting you to fail. Kids who grow up like that fail because that's what's expected of them. They're never given an even playing field. They're told they're losers from day one, and that's all they ever aspire to be."

Taylor didn't realize she'd gone on a tangent until Darby reached out.

Resting her hand on Taylor's forearm, she gently said, "We didn't mean to act like that toward your brother. Did we?" she asked, looking at Jade.

Jade shook her head, and Taylor felt guilty for lashing out. However, she didn't apologize. What she'd said was true. Every word. And whether Jade and Darby intended to treat Lonnie like that or not, they had.

Frowning, Taylor looked out at the water and realized she'd done the same thing. Even if she hadn't verbalized it. The disappointment she felt over her little brother and his lack of motivation to better himself was growing every day. He'd refused to discuss getting his mechanic's certificate any more than they'd discussed at La Cocina. Whenever she tried to teach him something new on the job site, he blew her off or joked around until she got frustrated and told him he was wasting her time.

And twice now, he'd asked for an advance on his paycheck. She'd refused both times and would continue to refuse. Something told her he was waiting to get a little cash in his hand so he could disappear. She was going to do what she could to keep him around, to give herself a little more time to break through the damage their mother had done to him and teach him what it meant to have a work ethic. If that meant withholding his pay until it was actually due to him, then she would.

She wasn't going to give him an easy out. Grandpa had always been toughest on the guys he believed in. Whether she believed in Lonnie because he deserved it or because she really just needed him to be the family she'd been craving, she was determined to believe in him. She believed he could be and do better for himself than looking for the easy outs Susan had always taken.

"Earth to Taylor," Darby sang.

Taylor blinked and gave her head a soft shake. "Sorry. What?"

"I asked if you were laying claim to Finn or could I have a go."

Wincing, Taylor crinkled her nose and twisted her mouth. "Ew. What?"

"Well, if you want him, I won't make a move."

Jade chuckled. "Friends don't hit on the guy their friend wants to hit on. What about Noah, Darby? You spent a week texting us about how much you'd missed him, then you slipped out in the middle of the night. Now you want a go at Finn?"

"My life is in Chammont Point," Darby stated with confidence. "I need a man who is in Chammont Point. I adore Noah, but he chose his career over our relationship, and I have to let him go. I can't ask him to come back here, and I don't want to go there. It's time to let my little bird fly." She held her hands up as if releasing a chickadee or something. But then she batted her long lashes at Taylor. "Finn's adorable. So I understand if he's off limits."

"Oh," Taylor muttered as she shook her head. "Go for it. He's yours."

"Really?" Jade asked, sounding like Taylor had pissed all over her parade. "You're not even the slightest bit interested in Finn?"

Heaving a sigh, Taylor frowned. "Don't you think I have enough problems right now?"

"Fair enough," Jade said.

Darby rubbed her hands together. "Sweet. I'm going to teach that man all kinds of things."

Taylor chuckled and glanced at Jade. Jade forced one of those sympathetic smiles that Taylor hated as much as she appreciated. She understood why Jade was concerned about her. But she wished her friend would back off a little. If Taylor was going to emotionally crash and burn, she'd rather not take everyone down with her.

As Taylor returned to work after her lunch break, she spotted Lonnie and Finn standing in the yard, nose to nose. There was an obvious confrontation going down that looked to be about one more snide comment from being a fist fight. She wasn't surprised. Actually, she was shocked it had taken three entire days to get to this point. The tension between the men had been at the breaking point since Lonnie had started.

Taylor didn't bother to figure out why. She wasn't interested in why. As the foreman, she had to be more focused on the underlying tensions between the two members of her crew and doing her best to keep them away from each other.

She turned off her ignition and hopped out of the truck.

"What's with you spying on me?" Lonnie screamed at Finn. "You're not my boss!"

"You're lucky in that," Finn yelled. "I'd fire you! Your sister's too good to you. Don't you have any pride? She's giving you a chance to prove yourself, and you're blowing it! Now give me my fucking tools back."

"Hey," she yelled when Lonnie pushed Finn. Finn pushed back as Taylor trotted up to them. She put herself between them and pressed a hand to each man's chest. "What the hell is going on?"

"He stole my tools," Finn explained as he glared at Lonnie. "I left them in the bedroom closet when I went to check out an apartment. They're gone now."

Lonnie smirked in a way that made Taylor want to smack him. That was a serious accusation, one that she didn't think Finn would make without cause, and Lonnie was blowing it off.

"Fuck you," Lonnie said. "I didn't take shit."

"Then let me check your car," Finn volleyed back, as if they'd covered this territory several times before Taylor had arrived.

Lonnie shook his head at Taylor. "I don't have to let him do shit. Tell him."

Taylor's stomach knotted. Rather than immediately taking Finn's side, even though something told her he was right, she did her best to stay neutral.

She looked at Finn. "You checked everywhere inside?"

"I don't set my tools down just anywhere."

"You checked?" she asked again. When he didn't answer, she nodded toward the house. "Go look around again. You're not going to accuse someone of stealing until you've verified that things are actually missing and not misplaced."

He narrowed his eyes at Lonnie for a few heartbeats before turning and stomping his way inside.

Taylor lowered her hand and faced her brother. "Did you take his tools?"

Snorting, Lonnie rolled his head back. "Are you serious?"

"Hey," she stated, suddenly not concerned about hurting his feelings, "you have a track record, so don't act like this is out of nowhere. I'm going to give you one chance to be honest and make things right. Did you take his tools?"

"No," he stated, still acting like she had no right to ask. "I didn't take the shithead's tools. He's had it out for me from day one, Taylor. You know that. You've seen it. He probably stole his own tools to get rid of me."

"Oh, come on," Taylor said. "He isn't going to go through that kind of trouble to get rid of you. He could walk away from this job and find another one without a problem."

"Yeah, except he wouldn't because he's been trying to get into your pants since—"

"That's enough," Taylor said firmly. Not only was she offended by the accusation that one of her crew would try that, but it wasn't true. Finn hadn't done a damn thing to try to woo Taylor. Finn had never crossed that line, and for Lonnie to imply it pissed her off. Finn had been respectful of her role from day one, which was a hell of a lot more than she could say for pretty much any other man who had worked for her.

Including Lonnie.

Finn stormed back outside. "They're not there." He stopped right in front of Lonnie again. "What did you do with my shit?"

Lonnie smirked. "I told you. I didn't touch your shit."

"Give me your keys." Taylor held her hand out and gestured for Lonnie to hand them over.

He narrowed his dark eyes at her for a moment before shoving his hand in his pocket and dropping his key chain into her hand. Taylor walked around him and hit the button on his remote to unlock the car. She opened the front passenger door and gave the area a quick glance. Then she moved to the backseat. Nothing.

Opening his trunk, she shifted the contents around. No tools.

"Fuckin' told you," Lonnie said.

Taylor closed the trunk and faced her brother. "Empty your pockets."

As soon as she said it, his already pale skin lost a few more shades, and the cocky look on his face disappeared. His mouth sagged and his eyes widened slightly as he stammered out, "W-What?"

Her heart dropped at his reaction. That was guilt if she'd ever seen it. That was the look of someone about to get caught doing exactly what they'd been denying. Goddamn it.

"Empty your pockets," she said more slowly. When he didn't move, she pressed her lips together and exhaled a shaky breath as a sense of dejection settled over her.

She'd spent so much time defending him to Jade and Darby. She'd snapped at Jade for not giving him a fair chance, and the worthless punk hadn't made it a week before proving Taylor wrong.

She was on the verge of losing her temper. She was about to freak out on the little thief, but she didn't want to lower herself to that level.

He wasn't worth the energy she would expend screaming and yelling. He wasn't worth the shame and guilt she'd feel afterward.

Shoving her hand toward him, she said, "Give me the receipt, Lonnie."

He didn't move. Didn't speak.

"You seem to have forgotten," Taylor said calmly, "I learned how to steal the same place you did—The School of Susan O'Shea. I remember helping her carry stuff she'd stolen into a pawnshop. So yeah, I do know what you did here." Staring into his eyes, so he made no mistake of how serious she was, she stated, "Give me the receipt, or I'll call the fucking cops myself."

After blowing out a breath, he pulled his wallet from his back pocket and produced a folded sheet of paper. Taylor opened it. The top gave the name of the pawnshop, and each line listed a different tool and how much Lonnie had gotten for them.

He'd stolen. Again.

He'd done the one thing she told him she could never forgive. Again.

Only this time, he'd stolen from someone that she'd taken responsibility for. Finn was her crew member. She was the foreman. This was her site. Her responsibility. And Lonnie had just shit all over her, her employee, and her job.

That was the final straw. That relationship she'd hoped for? Brother-sister? Not gonna happen.

She handed the receipt to Finn. "Is that everything?"

As he skimmed the list, the muscles in his jaw flexed with obvious anger. "Yeah."

"Where's the money?" she asked Lonnie.

"Taylor," Lonnie started, sagging his shoulders and giving her a sad look.

"Where's the fucking money, Lonnie?"

"I spent it," he muttered.

Taylor shook her head then focused on Finn. "Do you want to press charges?"

"Taylor," Lonnie repeated as if shocked that she'd even consider it.

Finn seemed to weigh her question for a moment before asking, "Is he fired?"

"Yeah," Taylor said, as if Lonnie weren't standing there, "he's fired."

"You kicking him out of your house?"

She nodded as she looked at her brother. "Yeah. I am kicking him out."

"Then no. That's good enough for me," Finn said.

"Fuck you both," Lonnie said. "Give me my keys."

Taylor held them up as she stared at him. "You go to my place. You get your shit. And you hit the road. Don't you ever come back."

Lonnie stared at her for a few moments, as if he couldn't believe she'd said that. He shoved his hand out, palm up. "You owe me pay for this week."

"I'll use it to buy back Finn's tools," she responded without hesitation.

Shaking his head, Lonnie let out a flat laugh. "Mom's right about you," he said with a venomous tone, "you're a fucking stuck-up bitch."

Taylor didn't let his words hit her. Like she gave a damn about what a couple of lowlifes like Lonnie and Susan O'Shea thought about her. Finn, however, took a step in Lonnie's direction as her brother spun on his feet and stormed toward his car like a petulant little child.

"Don't," Taylor said. "He isn't worth the trouble. I'm sorry," she said quietly. "For all of this."

"You don't have to—"

Turning, she shut him up with a hard shake of her head. "I vouched for him. Even though we all knew what he was like. That was my choice. And it was the wrong one."

"Taylor—"

"Go home, Finn. We're calling it a day." She took the receipt from his hand and looked at it before sighing. "I'll go get your tools and have them for you tomorrow."

"*Taylor*," Finn said more insistently.

"Go home." She couldn't listen to whatever he was going to say. Nothing he said would go over well, whether he intended to say *I told you so* or *I'm so sorry*. "I'm going to do a quick inventory, then I'll get to the pawnshop."

Walking into the reno house, she slammed the door behind her and looked around.

That stupid little shit. That goddamned fool. She'd given him a second chance. She'd handed him an opportunity to better himself, and he blew it.

The sad thing was that she wasn't surprised. Somewhere deep inside, she'd known all along her attempt at being a sister to Lonnie was going to end like this. Actually, it wasn't even somewhere deep inside. She'd known, but she'd chosen to ignore the facts because she was so determined to...what? Prove something? To whom? Why?

She'd been so desperate to have someone to call family, to have that so-called unbreakable bond, that she'd set herself, her company, and her brother up to fail. Jade had seen it coming. So had Darby. And Liam. And Finn. But Taylor had chosen to cling to hope.

Her grandfather would shake his head and mutter something about her being foolish before lighting a cigarette and shuffling off. He'd be disappointed in her. Almost as much as she was disappointed in herself.

"Hey," Finn said, coming into the living room behind her. She turned. The look on his face implied he wanted to comfort her or some other stupid shit that she didn't need. "I looked around when I was checking for my tools. I didn't see anything else missing. I think he took mine to make a point."

She nodded. She wouldn't put that past Lonnie. He'd known from the start that Finn didn't trust him. "I'm heading to the pawnshop, then. I doubt they've had time to put your tools out, but I won't risk them selling them."

"I can go."

"It's my responsibility. I'll swing by on my way home. I don't want to give him a chance to steal anything else."

"I'll go with you," Finn offered.

Taylor scoffed. "No, you won't." She softened her defensive posture when she saw the concern in his eyes. "I can take care of myself. Lock up on your way out. I'll see you tomorrow."

She left before she let his concern unhinge her more than she already was. She wasn't going to let anyone see how bad this hurt. However, the humiliation had started to set in, and she needed to be alone.

Twenty minutes later, she was explaining to the pawnshop owner that someone had stolen tools from her site. The owner wasn't impressed. She was given two options: buy the tools back at the regular price or file a claim at the police department and have the tools confiscated and locked up as evidence.

And have Lonnie arrested and locked up as a thief.

Taylor chose to buy back what had been stolen. But she did consider the second option for several seconds. Lonnie deserved to be arrested. He deserved to have charges filed against him. He deserved to do another stint in jail.

But she didn't have the energy to go down that path. Instead, she'd used her personal "emergency only" card to pay for Finn's tools and set things right with him.

Setting things right with Finn and getting Lonnie out of her life was worth the financial hit.

She wasn't surprised that Jade's car was parked in front of her house when she'd arrived within fifteen minutes of leaving the pawn shop. No doubt Finn rattled off to Jade and Liam about how Lonnie had pawned his tools.

Taylor walked in and frowned when she found Jade and Darby cleaning up. This wasn't Taylor's mess. She might not ever be accused of being a neat freak, but she wasn't a slob either. The couch must have been overturned by the way the cushions weren't sitting quite right. The end table looked like it'd been knocked over as well. The lamp shade was torn, probably from hitting the floor.

Lonnie had trashed the place before leaving. She wasn't surprised.

"Sorry," Jade said without any prompting. Her sad eyes didn't hold judgment or even an ounce of *I told you so*. Just sympathy. "I'm so sorry, Taylor."

She shook her head and looked around at the mess. Lonnie's bag was gone. So was her television, wireless speaker, and the laptop that she rarely used. A wry laugh left her when she turned and noticed the hole in the wall next to the front door. From the placement, he must have punched it on his way out.

Rolling her head back, she looked at the ceiling and blew out a long breath.

"I'll call Finn over. He can fix it," Jade offered.

"No. I have drywall patches and putty in my truck."

"Let Finn fix it," Darby said softly. "You shouldn't—"

"It's my mess," Taylor stated, cutting her off. "So is this. What are you guys doing here?"

"Finn told us what happened, so we wanted to check on you," Darby said. She pouted as she looked around at the destruction. "Oh, boo."

Taylor lifted her hand to put a stop to the pity. "Don't. I knew I was making a mistake. But I had to try." She swallowed hard as she felt heartache creeping up on her. "I had to try. And I did. And...now I know. I know without a doubt, I'm better off without them." She looked at the couch again. "Thanks for cleaning up what you have. I'll get the rest."

"Taylor," Jade started.

She looked at the hole in the wall again. It would take her half an hour to fix the hole and then a few minutes to paint over the patch. Lonnie would have known she'd do the work herself. He probably wanted to make it harder for her to get over kicking him out. Having him act like a petty ass only made it easier.

The work wasn't the issue. His lack of respect was.

Sure, she was just renting the house. But it was still her house. And someone trashing her house pissed her off, probably even more than a few missing electronics.

She reached into her pocket and fingered the pawnshop

receipt. Would Lonnie be stupid enough to go back to the same shop to pawn her laptop? No, if he had, they probably would have run into each other since she'd spent so long trying to get Finn's tools back.

That realization brought another with it—he had stolen from his ex. He had pawned her items. And he was going to pawn Taylor's too.

"I'm sorry that I dragged you guys into my mess," she said, and finally, her composure broke, and her voice cracked.

"It's okay," Jade said, picking up a pillow and putting it back on the couch.

"It's not," Taylor said. "You warned me."

"Because I didn't want you to get hurt."

"Taylor," Darby said in an unusually serious tone. "We love you. We know you had to try. We understand. Please don't blame yourself."

"What I don't get," Jade said, "is why he would do that. Why would he steal three days into working for you? It couldn't have been more obvious who had done it."

"Because I was putting expectations on him," Taylor said sadly. "I was pushing him. I wasn't going to stand by and watch him do nothing with his life. He didn't like that. He was going to show me that I can't tell him what to do." She scoffed as she looked around. "My grandfather said the real reason my mom took off the way she did was because after my grandma died, he refused to indulge her. He refused to let her get away with the things my grandma did. Once he put rules into place, she started rebelling."

"Some people don't like rules," Darby offered.

"Some people would rather fail than follow the rules," Taylor said. "Looks like Lonnie is one of them."

"Well, he's stupid," Jade offered. "Because he blew the best chance he was ever going to get. The chance that you gave him."

Taylor drew a deep breath. "The last chance I'm ever going to give him." Sadness washed over her, not at the state of her home or even the fact that he'd stolen from her, but because he'd rather be a grifter than accept a helping hand. He'd rather be a crook and a liar than have to put in an honest day of work. He'd rather walk away than try to learn how to be a brother.

The saddest thing, Taylor had come to realize, was that she'd allowed herself to hope that she was wrong about him. She'd *wanted* to be wrong about him. She'd wanted to have a brother, and she was willing to overlook the obvious in order to have one. That had been foolish.

Fool me once, her grandfather used to say, *shame on you. Fool me twice, shame on me.*

"This is why I don't trust people," she said without thinking. "This is why I don't let anyone in."

"You let us in," Jade said softly.

Taylor had to swallow as her chest grew heavy. "Yeah. I did."

"We'll never make you regret it," Darby promised. "We're going to take care of you."

With a forced smile on her lips, Taylor nodded. "I know. I'm really glad I have you guys. But, um, I need you to go now."

"No," Jade whispered.

"This is my mess, and I need to clean it up." She wasn't

talking about the scattered items on the floor or the hole Lonnie put in the wall. And they all knew it.

"Call us," Darby said as she squeezed Taylor's hand. "Please. Call us."

"I will."

Jade gave Taylor a big hug before looking at her with sad eyes. She didn't say anything, though. She understood that if she did, she'd make things worse.

Once her friends were gone, Taylor eased down on the sofa and looked around her place. She was angry—at herself and at Lonnie, but if she were honest, part of her was relieved. Now that he'd proven himself to be no better than she'd expected, she could let go of the idea that she had a family out there somewhere. She could stop being angry at a mother who didn't want her. She could let go of a brother who didn't deserve her.

Lonnie had proven who he really was, but Taylor had proven herself too. She'd proven that underneath her tough exterior she was a caring person. She'd proven that she could be kind and considerate and caring. That was so much more than she'd ever given herself credit for.

Despite the hurt and humiliation and the mess around her, Taylor smiled. The cost had been high, but she'd finally come to see the version of herself that Jade and Darby insisted was there.

FOURTEEN

THE FOLLOWING EVENING, Taylor sat at the table with Darby and Jade as she looked out over the calm water of the cove. She wished Jade and Darby would stop insisting she didn't have to apologize. Taylor's mistake had impacted them all. She *did* need to apologize, and she needed them to accept her apology instead of brushing it off.

"She's beating herself up again," Darby said with a stage whisper.

"She's always beating herself up," Jade responded with the same theatrical flare.

"You know what she needs," Darby responded.

"Harper's ice cream," she and Jade said in unison.

Despite her dark mood, Taylor smiled. She had known exactly what they were going to say. Their friendship had turned into one of those where they finished each other's thoughts. She'd always found it annoying when other people did that, but now there was comfort in the habit. They had all rubbed off on each other a long time ago, but now they seemed to be merging into one. For some reason that she didn't fully understand, Taylor found comfort in that.

Family. That's what Jade had called it when Darby pointed out that they had started speaking over each other and laughing when they knew what the other was going to say. *That's what families do*, she said. Jade would know that better than Darby and Taylor. Jade had always been surrounded by family, and they were much closer than most.

Taylor hadn't had that kind of familial connection, but still, she couldn't disagree. She'd finished her grandfather's thoughts thousands of times before he'd died. And he was still finishing her thoughts in her head, or telling her what he thought, whenever she was debating some issue.

"Not until you hear me out." Taylor eyed her friends across the table. "You guys warned me against going down this road, and I didn't listen. You were right about him. You guys were right about both of them—Lonnie and Mom."

"I wish we hadn't been," Jade said softly.

"Listen," Darby stated, "you wanted a relationship with your family. We understand that."

"But my family is shit," Taylor said lightly.

"No, they aren't," Jade said, "because we're your family. And we aren't shit. Well…I'm not, I can't speak for her." She grinned as she gestured toward Darby.

"Oh, screw you," Darby said with mock offense.

"I am sorry that I dragged you into this mess, and I am asking that you accept my apology so I can try to start letting go of the guilt that's eating me alive."

"Apology accepted," Jade said.

"Completely accepted," Darby added.

Taylor laughed softly. She loved them. She really did. "Thank you," she said. "What was that about ice cream? Harper's sounds perfect."

The three of them stood but hadn't even walked away from the table before Liam let out a loud whistle that echoed around the cove. They all turned toward the small cabin he shared with Jade. He waved them over as Finn stepped behind him, as if to verify they heard Liam's obnoxious sound.

"Guys," Liam called from the doorway. "You need to come in here. Now."

A sense of dread washed over Taylor. She didn't know what could have happened, but something in her gut told her she didn't want to know. He had an odd look in his eyes as she neared him, and when she met his gaze, he turned away.

"What is it?" Jade asked as they neared the cabin.

"Come in here," Liam said more gently.

Taylor felt like she was walking through mud. For reasons she couldn't understand, fear settled over her. When she finally got to the cabin, the look on Finn's face told her all she needed to know. He lifted his hand as if to stop her but then nodded at the television screen, which was paused on a newscaster with her mouth open and her eyes half closed.

"I think..." Finn started and then frowned.

"Taylor," Liam said gently, "you need to see this."

Finn hit a button on the remote, and the newscaster started talking again.

Taylor only heard the first few words about a convenience store robbery the previous afternoon. Then, as soon as video of the crime filled the screen, her heartbeat drowned out the rest of the sound. The quality of the security camera wasn't great, but she immediately recognized the criminal.

There, holding a gun, was her brother robbing a clerk. As he took cash from the register, the number for the anonymous tip line filled the bottom of the screen.

"Oh, shit," Darby said softly.

"Son of a bitch," Jade whispered.

"That's him, right?" Finn asked. "That's Lonnie."

Taylor nodded because she couldn't find her voice.

"I'll call it in," Liam said quietly after several moments of silence hung over them.

"No," Taylor finally managed to say. Though her mouth was dry and her chest tight, she pulled her phone from her pocket. "He's my brother. I'll make the call."

"Tay," Darby said sympathetically.

Taylor ignored her, then excused herself to take the phone outside. She couldn't bear the thought of her closest friends—her chosen family—watching her turn in her biological brother for a crime she wasn't the least bit surprised that he'd been filmed committing.

Shame filled her chest and made her heart pound when someone answered the tip line. But the shame wasn't because she was turning in her brother, or even because Lonnie was her brother. Her shame was because she'd brought him into their lives. She'd invited him to stay. She'd given him reason to stay. And this was what he'd done.

And he'd done it not just to her and Finn and her friends who owned ReDo, but to her new hometown. This was the place where she had started to set down roots, where she was determined to build a successful business. Chammont Point was the town she'd grown to love as her own.

"Hello?" the voice on the other end of the call said for a second time.

"Hi," Taylor said with a strained voice, "I just saw footage of a convenience store robbery on the news."

"Do you have information on the crime?"

Taylor was glad that she'd stepped outside when she closed her eyes and a tear fell down her cheek. "Yeah," she said, "I do."

After hanging up with the tip line, Taylor walked directly to her truck and headed home. She wasn't ready to have her friends give her sympathy or reassurances or whatever they intended to do. Lonnie committed armed robbery. She'd had no choice but to turn him in.

She didn't need sympathy. She needed space. She needed to clear her head.

She needed her grandpa to give her a kick in the pants to pick herself up and get over it. Since she didn't have him any longer, she did the next best thing. She walked out onto the back porch with a cup and a pack of smokes.

Within minutes, Taylor was sitting in the rocking chair on her back porch as the scents of cigarette smoke and black coffee wafted in the breeze. Memories of her grandfather filled her mind as she stared out at her backyard. Now that she'd given her information to the police, an unexpected peace found her. If they'd done nothing else for her, Susan and Lonnie had finally convinced her she no longer needed blood bonds to feel complete.

Taylor never would have thought she'd come to a point when she could stop resenting the tough love approach her grandfather had taken, but seeing the world through his eyes—thanks to her misguided attempt at saving Lonnie—had given her a new perspective. She had tried so hard to help him find the right path. She'd come too close to sacrificing all the hard work and all the things she'd overcome to help him.

Her grandfather had been right about so many things. Including when he'd insisted that she was better off without her mother. That applied to her brother too.

With that realization, Taylor felt a punch to her gut. An unexpected sob welled in her chest and rushed out before she could stop it. Tears filled her eyes as grief surrounded her like a storm cloud. The only family she'd ever known, the only family she'd ever had, was gone. The only man she'd ever been able to count on had died.

Though it'd been four years since her grandfather passed, she suddenly felt the loss as much as she had as she'd watched him take his last ragged breath. She'd held his hand that day. She hadn't done that since she was a young child. They had never been affectionate, but as he'd struggled to take his last inhalations, she'd grasped his hands in hers and whispered words of encouragement.

She'd told him that it was okay to let go. She'd told him to go in peace. She'd told him it was time to rest.

The thing she hadn't told him was that she'd loved him. But she did. She'd loved him so much that it had scared her. She'd never let herself feel the depth of her love for him because her fear had always run deeper. The fear that he'd abandon her was always there, always overshadowing everything else.

Though she hadn't wanted to hang on to what her mother had taught her, she had learned that having someone leave her was much easier if she wasn't overly attached. So Taylor had never let him in. Not really. And now he was gone.

She hated that she'd never let herself trust him enough to love him the way that a grandfather deserved to be loved. She'd resented him for so many reasons, but looking back, those reasons were excuses not to get close to him.

She couldn't fix that now. She couldn't change the distance she'd kept between them.

And her heart shattered knowing that she would never be able to tell him that she loved him.

So many times when she thought of her grandfather, she thought of his gruff voice and blunt advice. This time, however, she thought of all the things he'd done to help her grow into the person she'd become. All the times he'd taken the time to teach her about building things and how to safely handle tools. When she'd bought her first car, he'd taught her how to change a tire and check the oil. When she'd told him she'd had her first date, he'd taught her how to land a punch in case the boy got frisky.

All those things, at the time, had seemed so extreme, but now she understood what that was. He never said he loved her either, but he'd shown her in a thousand different ways. He'd been a rock in her life, and she was only realizing how much that had meant to her.

She'd give anything to tell him that. She'd give anything

to tell him she understood now and appreciated him now. And she loved him.

She loved him so damn much.

Curling her legs to her chest, Taylor hugged herself and, finally, for the first time since losing him, she grieved for her grandfather.

FIFTEEN

AS SHE DROVE to the cove a week later, with the local morning news playing on the radio, Taylor heard that Lonnie had been spotted at a cheap motel in Indianapolis and had been arrested.

Of course, at first, she felt guilt for that. She'd been the one to give his name to the police tip line, after all. But once the guilt eased, she'd come to realize—even without Jade and Darby reassuring her that she'd done the right thing—that Lonnie was the only person responsible for his current situation.

He'd robbed a convenience store. At gunpoint. He could have ended up killing the clerk. Getting arrested was nobody's fault but his own.

Carrying a drink holder with one black coffee, one iced mocha, and a green tea, Taylor hopped out of her truck and headed toward the little table in the cove. Peace washed over her as it did every time she came to this place. No wonder she spent so much time here.

The problems of the world seemed to fade as she headed

toward her favorite spot: the table nestled in the safety of the cove.

"Good morning," she said to Darby, who was already at the table with a scattering of paint samples.

"You're late."

"There was a line at the coffee shop."

Darby looked up and grinned. "You know, it used to be a lot more fun picking on you. You barely even pick back these days."

Easing down into her chair, Taylor smiled. "I know. It's odd."

"You're odd," Darby said.

"Says the girl with a neon-green scarf tied around her neck."

Darby smiled as she accepted her drink. "Thank you. I needed that comeback. I've missed your usual snarky self."

Taylor shrugged. "What can I say? I'm not as angry with the world these days."

"Why's that?"

A slight warmth covered her cheeks, and she imagined her pale skin was flushing. "I just... For so long, I felt like a discarded piece of trash by my mom. Now I know."

"She's the trash," Darby said.

Taylor nodded. "Without a doubt."

"So is that garbage brother of yours."

"*Half*-brother," Taylor clarified. "And I don't even think I'm going to give him that title any longer. He was arrested by the way."

"Good," Darby stated before taking a drink from her straw. "You don't need him coming around."

"No, I don't. Being an only child wasn't that bad. Where's Jade?"

Darby lowered the samples she'd been debating and looked off in the distance. "She and Liam haven't come back from their morning trip out on the lake. They only took one canoe. They never go out in one canoe. Something's up," she said with narrowed eyes as if that would help her sort out the situation.

Taylor eyed her. "You think something's up because they took one canoe instead of two?"

"I have a feeling." Darby danced her fingers over her chest. "Like swan bumps on my soul."

"Swan bumps on your…" Taylor didn't finish. Even if she asked for clarification, she knew she'd just get some oddball Darbyism. Swan bumps on her soul. Probably something akin to goosebumps on a normal person's skin, but Darby wasn't normal. Darby was…Darby. Being Darby was enough for her, and Taylor was content to let it be enough for her too.

Darby's off-the-wall humor had become so refreshing for Taylor. She didn't used to feel that way. She used to worry that Darby would be singled out because of her oddball way of seeing and doing things. However, after all the things they'd been through, Taylor had grown to appreciate the unique approach Darby took to living.

She'd even come to appreciate Jade's maternal nurturing. They really did balance each other out. The three of them. They shouldn't work. In another life, another time and place, they probably wouldn't. But fate or some other force had brought them together, and everything fit.

Taylor was so grateful for that.

"Oh, they're back," Darby said, holding her hand to her forehead to shield her eyes as she peered out over the cove.

Thankful for the distraction from her deep thoughts, Taylor watched Liam row the canoe across the water like there was no resistance. Within minutes, they were close enough that she could see the smile on Jade's face.

"Yeah. Something was up, but I don't think we want to know what it was."

Darby giggled as Jade practically jumped from the canoe the moment it was close enough to shore. Taylor cocked a brow at the clumsy movements of her friend. If Jade was a drinker, Taylor would wonder if she'd been hitting the bottle. But, since Jade was perpetually sober, she couldn't be tipsy. She squealed as she rushed toward them.

A moment later, Darby gasped and sat taller.

"What?" Taylor asked.

"He proposed," Jade yelled in a high-pitched tone that sounded like a teenager who'd been asked to the prom by her dream date. Holding out her hand, Jade flashed an engagement ring. "He proposed. I didn't have to. *He* did."

Darby jumped up, joining in the cheerleader-esque excitement. They started talking so fast that Taylor couldn't keep up. She stood, knowing she should take part if for no other reason than Jade would want her to. She smiled brightly and looked at the ring as she offered her congratulations. Liam finally had the canoe secure enough to join them. He wrapped his arm around Jade's shoulders and kissed her head.

"Did you tell her?" he asked.

"That you got engaged?" Darby asked. "Did you not hear her squealing?"

"No, the other thing," Liam said and nodded toward Taylor.

As always, as soon as she realized she was out of the loop on something, insecurity flared in her mind. Not just insecurity but fear that she'd done something wrong.

However, Darby giggled and draped her arm around Taylor's shoulders. "Nope. I was waiting for you guys."

"What's going on?" Taylor asked hesitantly.

"Well..." Darby drawled out in her usual dramatic fashion. "The thing is..."

Jade clasped her hands together and brought them to her chest, causing light to reflect off the diamond on her finger. "We agreed to sell enough of our property to squeeze another tiny house between us. You're moving to the cove."

Widening her eyes, Taylor looked from Jade to Darby to Liam. "What?"

He nodded, and Taylor spun to look at the common area between their houses. "There isn't room."

"Of course there is, silly," Darby said. She made a grand, sweeping gesture with her hand. "See, we got it all worked out. We move the fire pit forward a little bit, you build your house back a little bit, and then we all live happily ever after being besties *and* neighbors! For-*ever*."

Darby was right. Taylor wasn't her usual snarky self. She usually would have had a sarcastic comeback, something about how she couldn't imagine living next to Darby forever. But instead, her heart swelled, and her throat tightened. They were making room for her. And that wasn't just at the dining room table or around the fire pit. They were selling off property to make room for her.

"Wow," she whispered.

"Is that a good wow?" Jade asked.

Taylor quickly wiped her cheeks before turning and letting a huge smile curve her lips. "Yeah. That's a good wow."

"So, you're on board?" Liam asked.

Laughing lightly, Taylor nodded. "Oh, yeah. You bitches are never getting rid of me now."

"Yay!" Darby yelled before swooping in to hug Taylor. Jade bounced her way to them and hugged them both. That was nice, but then Liam wrapped all three into a big bear hug and squeezed.

"No," Taylor groaned despite the love filling her heart. "This is too much affection. I'm melting!"

Between making plans for her new home and helping Jade and Darby plan the perfect outdoor wedding, Taylor barely had time to think about Lonnie or Susan. Before she knew it, it was spring again, and it began with an intimate ceremony on the cove. Taylor never would have imagined she'd enjoy the role of bridesmaid, but being pulled into the pre-wedding activities that Darby obsessed over had been exactly what she'd needed to prevent her from slipping back to old habits.

Lonnie had pleaded guilty, Taylor suspected to get a lesser punishment. Her brother was in prison now, and that had taken an emotional toll on her, even though she had written him off. The shame of being related to yet another convicted thief hadn't stung nearly as much with her best friends there to prevent her from focusing on the damage he'd done. Instead, she'd put her energy into designing her home, buying the right materials, and building her new life in the cove.

Now, with the sun setting over the calm water and the exchange of vows finished, Taylor sipped her beer as she watched Jade and Liam share a slow dance on the beach. She was happy for Jade. Their lives were all changing so fast. That used to terrify Taylor. That part of her that feared the unknown hadn't gone away completely, but she was learning to focus on the good.

"Don't look so stressed," Darby said, sliding up next to her. She sipped from the bright pink straw sticking out between an umbrella, a stack of fruit on a spike, and a miniature bottle of tequila turned upside down.

"I'm not stressed."

"Of course you are. That's what you do."

Taylor smiled wistfully when Liam spun Jade then pulled her back in. "I really am happy for them. It's just that...things will be different now."

"Not really."

"She has a husband now."

"She's had him hanging off her arm for two years now, Tay. Marrying him won't change anything."

"Hanging off her arm?" she asked in an attempt to change the subject.

"Yeah," Darby said with a shrug. "Liam is like an accessory. Like a fancy purse or a brooch."

"I think he'd disagree," Taylor said.

She gently nudged Taylor. "We know the truth. Jade isn't going anywhere. We three cannot be separated. We're family.

Especially now." She turned and gestured toward the new house nestled in the cove.

Taylor's place was small, even compared to Darby's and Jade's little cabins, but she still thought it was perfect. She didn't need much space. She didn't *want* much space. She preferred sitting outside anyway, here in the cove. Spring was here, birds were chirping, and watching the sun set over the water had become her favorite part of the day. Everything here brought peace to her soul.

"Oh, excuse me." Darby winked at Taylor before walking away with a shitty grin on her lips.

Taylor didn't even have to wonder why. Every time Finn was anywhere near Taylor, Darby winked and nudged and giggled. Darby had barely walked away before Finn took her place. Ever since Finn had nicely but firmly let Darby know he wasn't interested in any kind of relationship—long or short term—with her, Darby had jumped on the Taylor and Finn bandwagon. Not that there was a bandwagon.

"Nice wedding, huh?" he asked.

"Yeah," Taylor said. "It was."

"Your house looks great," he continued.

"Thanks."

"Whoever helped you put up that wood siding must have been a real stud."

She grinned despite her intention to blow him off. "Oh, I don't think I'd go that far, but he had a pulse, so that's something."

As always, he rolled his head back, and that obnoxious laugh of his ripped through the cove. She hated that she'd come to appreciate that he laughed at her wry humor. Far too many people stared at her, not realizing she was teasing in her own dry way.

Finn got her, and Taylor liked that. She liked that he laughed at her jokes instead of taking offense. But she didn't have some great secret crush on him like Jade kept suggesting she should. Taylor and Finn had become friends, and that was all Taylor was interested in. She had too many complications to sort out before she went looking for more.

She'd come to terms that her mother and brother were useless. She'd realized her grandfather had been all the real family she'd ever needed as a child. And, more than that, she'd started to find a way to feel comfortable with her past.

She didn't want to add any complications to all of that. Like with her jokes, Finn seemed to get that too. They had a comfortable relationship, but it wasn't more than friendship. Taylor wasn't convinced that it ever would be—even if Jade and Darby had other ideas for them.

Taylor returned her attention to the small gathering when Darby tapped a spoon against her glass. The cove grew quiet as she stood tall and proud.

"Before the bride and groom cut the cake," Darby said, "it's speech time." She reached into her cleavage and pulled out a piece of paper, causing laughs to fill the air. The smile on her bright-red lips made it clear she'd gotten the reaction she'd been seeking. After clearing her throat and unfolding the paper, she read what she'd written—a long, sometimes funny, recollection of how she and Taylor had forced Jade to accept Liam's undying love. She ended by eying Liam and giving him a lighthearted warning about doing right by her friend…or else.

Turning, Darby looked at Taylor and nodded slightly.

Oh. It was Taylor's turn. Shit.

She inhaled deeply as she looked around at the expectant faces. Parker Alonso, Liam's employee, stood with her little girl on her hip. Jade's boys had put their phones away long enough to pay attention. Finn smiled that stupid smile. Darby stood with her bright-red hair up in a fancy bun with her fruity drink ready to take part in the toast. And Liam stood with his arm around Jade's shoulders.

They were all watching her, waiting, and Taylor suddenly forgot the words she'd written to celebrate Jade and Liam's union. When she'd been trying to figure out what she was supposed to write, Darby kept telling her to write what was in her heart. Taylor kept telling her that wasn't helpful, but now, Taylor realized Darby had been right. All she had to say was what she was feeling, which sounded so trite she almost rolled her eyes.

Instead, Taylor lifted her glass, smiled, and said two words that expressed everything. "To family."

ALSO BY MARCI BOLDEN

Chammont Point Series:

The Restarting Point

The Selling Point

The Breaking Point

A Life Without Water Series:

A Life Without Water

A Life Without Flowers

A Life Without Regrets

Stonehill Series:

The Road Leads Back

Friends Without Benefits

The Forgotten Path

Jessica's Wish

This Old Cafe

Forever Yours

The Women of Hearts Series:

Hidden Hearts

Burning Hearts

Stolen Hearts

Secret Hearts

Other Titles:

California Can Wait

Seducing Kate

The Rebound

ABOUT THE AUTHOR

As a teen, Marci Bolden skipped over young adult books and jumped right into reading romance novels. She never left.

Marci lives in the Midwest with her husband, kiddos, and numerous rescue pets. If she had an ounce of willpower, Marci would embrace healthy living, but until cupcakes and wine are no longer available at the local market, she will appease her guilt by reading self-help books and promising to join a gym "soon."

Visit her here:
www.marcibolden.com

 facebook.com/MarciBoldenAuthor
 twitter.com/BoldenMarci
instagram.com/marciboldenauthor